BASIC SPANISH

• • •

Berlitz®

Berlitz Publishing Company, Inc., 400 Alexander Park, Princeton, NJ 08540-6306

Cover photograph — La Sagrada Familia, Barcelona, Spain

First English language edition – 1993

ISBN: 2–8315–6178-7

INTRODUCTION

Language Learning with Berlitz

Berlitz aims to help you acquire a practical knowledge of a new language as quickly and as naturally as possible.

A language is conveyed, first and foremost, by words. For over a hundred years, we have dedicated ourselves to the teaching of spoken language.

You are probably reading this introduction because you want to be able to enjoy communicating in Spanish – on vacation, for business or with friends and family. The most useful method of communication is the *spoken language*. It isn't enough to study the mechanics of a language. It's only by *speaking* a language that we can learn to communicate effectively.

It follows, then, that the most effective study program is one that gives you every possible chance to participate, to carry on a dialogue – in other words, *to speak*.

The Berlitz approach is based on a progressive discovery of the language through carefully selected "steps" arranged so that each one depends on the previous one, forming a chain of increasing difficulty. This way, you approach the new language with only the amount of knowledge that can be assimilated within a given time. Mastery of the language is thus achieved progressively and systematically.

BASIC SPANISH: A Dynamic, Self-Taught Course

This course will enable you to study Spanish at home – by yourself or with a friend. You will be able make progress immediately, without having to study pages and pages of rules!

Words or grammatical structures are translated only when they appear for the first time. In addition, English is limited to a narrow column in the margin of each page; the study sections contain only Spanish. We've done this so you won't get into the habit of translating everything you see or hear back into English.

The English explanations in the margins will help you to understand the Spanish text when you are unsure, but you should try not to rely on them too much. The margins can be easily covered with a piece of paper when you are following the Spanish text.

BASIC SPANISH avoids the use of numerous dull grammatical rules. Instead, BASIC SPANISH presents succinct explanations of points of grammar, expressed in clear, direct language that everyone can easily understand.

Contents of BASIC SPANISH

a) a book with texts, explanatory notes in English, and exercises in Spanish;

b) three hours of audio material containing recordings of the Spanish text.

Use of the Course

Here are a few tips to help you get the full benefit of BASIC SPANISH:

1. First listen to a scene without opening your book. Don't try to join in just yet.
2. Then listen again, following the scene in your book, right up to the audio end signal.
3. Go over the same scene, consulting the translation and marginal notes.
4. Go back to the first page of the scene. Listen again, repeating each sentence during the pause. Repeat this process until you don't need the book anymore.
5. Turn off the audio player and read aloud until you feel comfortable with the text.

Getting the most out of BASIC SPANISH

Here's how to get the best results as quickly as possible:

1. Set aside specific times for your Spanish studies. Allow for three one-hour study sessions per week. Remember that several short sessions at regular intervals are more effective than one longer session.
2. Be sure you master each section before moving on to the next. The program is based on a method of increasing levels of difficulty, so your ability to assimilate each new section will depend on how well you've mastered the previous ones. Study each section from beginning to end at least two or three times. The truth is, mastery of a language involves certain habits, so it can be gained only by repetition. It isn't enough to understand what you hear: you should feel comfortable and be able to answer quickly, without having to think in English first.
3. Always speak out loud. Your pronunciation mechanisms need to learn to move automatically in ways that are almost totally unfamiliar to you. Speaking involves a physical activity, so mental repetition or passive participation isn't enough.

4. Remember that making mistakes while you're learning is inevitable. *Everyone* make lots of mistakes when they're learning a new language, including children as they are assimilating their native tongue. Take advantage of your mistakes; use them as a learning tool.

5. Imitate the Spanish pronunciation as well as you can. Don't be afraid of saying something that doesn't sound right. It's only with practice that you'll be able to speak without sounding "funny" to a native speaker of Spanish. So imitate exactly the sounds and constructions you hear.

We wish you all the best and hope you'll find BASIC SPANISH not only helpful, but fun as well.

ESCENA 1

PRÓLOGO

Prologue

Juan ¡Shhh! ¡ *Escuche*!

¡Escuche **la música**!

Escuche …

un coche.

Un Chevrolet.

Un coche **americano.**

Y esto …

¡Escuche! – Listen! Notice the two exclamation marks, **¡** at the beginning of the sentence and **!** at the end.
música – Notice the accent on the first syllable! Spanish has one written accent (acute), and it shows the syllable you need to stress.

un coche – an automobile, a car
americano – American
You'll stress the next-to-last syllable. Unless another syllable has a written accent, this is the syllable usually stressed when a word ends in a vowel.
y – and
esto – this (invariable neuter form: neither masculine nor feminine)

es un Toyota.

Un coche **japonés.**

Repeat, following Juan's stress pattern: **un coche, una bicicleta.** Notice that the stress falls on the next-to-last syllable, as it does in these words too: **escuche, americano, Toyota.**

Repita: **el** Toyota es un coche japonés.

El **Chevrolet** es un coche americano.

Repita: a-me-ri-ca-no,

ja-po-nés.

Esto …

es **una bicicleta.**

Repita: un coche,

una bicicleta.

Un – una.

Un – una.

Un – una.

…

¡Ah! Es **Pedro**.

Y esto …

es **… un … reloj.**

Un reloj.

Repita **después de** Pedro:

Pedro: Uno.

Juan: *Repita*: uno.

un reloj – a watch. Listen carefully to the final sound, called **jota.** It's pronounced like a very strong **h,** well back in the throat.
después de – after
un, una – a, an (masculine and feminine articles in Spanish)
uno, una; dos; tres … – one; two; three …

Pedro	**Dos.**
Juan	Dos.
Pedro	**Tres.**
Juan	Tres.
Pedro	**Cuatro.**
Juan	Cuatro.
Pedro	**Cinco.**
Juan	Cinco.
Pedro	**Seis.**
Juan	Seis.
Pedro	**Siete.**
Juan	Siete.
	…
Pedro	**¡Las siete!**
	Ocho.
Juan	Ocho.
	…
Pedro	¡Las ocho!
	¡Son las ocho!
	Nueve.
Juan	Nueve.

The time of day
las siete – seven o'clock. The plural feminine article (**las**) goes before the number, because the noun **horas** is understood.
Son las ocho. – It's eight o'clock. The verb **be** is used to express time – in the singular for one o'clock, in the plural from two on – followed by the feminine article and the number.
Numbers from 4 to 9: **cuatro, cinco, seis, siete, ocho, nueve**

Pedro	Son las nueve.
	¿Las nueve? ¿Son las nueve?
	¡Ay! ¡Son las nueve!
	…
Sr. García	¡Entre!
Juan	Es **el profesor**, el Sr. García.

¡Entre! – Come in! Imperative of the verb **entrar** – to enter, to come in. The polite **you** is shown by the 3rd person. Think of the phrase "Madam is too kind."
el profesor – the teacher. Notice the single **s.** Such simplified spellings occur often in Spanish.

Sr. Gracía	**Sí …** ¡Entre!
	¡Ah! ¡Pedro!
Pedro	¡**Buenos días**! Buenos días, **señor**.
Sr. García	Buenos días, Pedro.
	¡Pedro! …
Pedro	¿Sí, señor?
Sr. García	¿Son las nueve?
Pedro	Sí, Sr. García, son las nueve.

¡Buenos días! – Good morning!
¿Son las nueve? – Is it nine o'clock? Notice the two question marks, **¿** at the beginning of the sentence and **?** at the end.
sí – yes

Juan	**Bueno.**
	Conteste: ¿Son las seis? – **No**, …
Juanita	– No, **no son** las seis.
	Repita: no, no son las seis.
Juan	*Conteste*: ¿ Son las siete? – No, no son …
Juanita	– No, no son las siete. *Repita*.
Juan	*Conteste*: ¡Son las ocho? – No, …

Juanita	– No, no son las ocho. *Repita*.	
Juan	*Conteste*: ¿**Qué hora** es? – Son las …	**¿Qué hora es?** – What time is it?
Juanita	– Son las nueve.	
Juan	**Perdón, …**	**Perdón.** – Excuse me.
	¿Qué hora?	
Juanita	– Las nueve.	**las nueve** – nine o'clock
Juan	¿Las nueve?	
Juanita	– Sí.	
Juan	¡Ah! **Gracias**.	**Gracias.** – Thank you.

•••

FIN DE LA **ESCENA 1**

Exercise 1

1. Read in Spanish:

1, 2, 3, 4, 5, 6, 7, 8, 9,
9, 8, 7, 6, 5, 4, 3, 2, 1,
1, 3, 5, 7, 9,
2, 4, 6, 8.

2. ¿Qué hora es?

3. ¿Qué hora es?

4. ¿Son las seis?
¿Qué hora es?

CORRECCIÓN.

1. Uno, dos, tres, cuatro, cinco, seis, siete, ocho, nueve,
Nueve, ocho, siete, seis, cinco, cuatro, tres, dos, uno.
Uno, tres, cinco, siete, nueve,
Dos, cuatro, seis, ocho.
2. Son las dos.
3. Son las cuatro.
4. No, no son las seis.
Son las siete.

ESCENA 2

ARITMÉTICA — Arithmetic

Juan	¡Shhh! *¡Escuche!*
	Escuche, **por favor:**
	Uno – dos, uno – dos, uno – dos, uno – dos
	…
	Repita: uno,
	dos,
	tres,

Escuche, por favor. – Please listen.
por favor – please
Repita. – Repeat. Imperative of the verb **repetir.**
Numbers from 1 to 3: **uno, dos, tres.**

Numbers from 4 to 12: **cuatro, cinco, seis, siete, ocho, nueve, diez**, **once**, **doce.**
Notice that the **c** in **once** and **doce** and the **z** in **diez** are pronounced alike. In Spain this sound is like the English **th** in **thin,** with the tip of the tongue between the teeth. But in Latin America the **s** sound is generally used instead.

cuatro,

cinco.

Repita: cinco, seis, siete,

ocho, nueve, **diez.**

Diez,

once,

doce.

Repita: diez, once, doce.

bueno – good (masculine)

Bueno.

ahora – now

Escuche a Pedro. – Listen to Pedro.
Escuche al profesor. – Listen to the teacher.
al = **a** + **el**

Ahora, *escuche* **a** Pedro y

escuche **al** profesor.

Sr. García — ¿Qué hora es?

Pedro — – Son las nueve y quince minutos.

el teléfono – the telephone. There is a written accent because the stress is not where you expect it to be – on the next-to-last syllable.

¡Oh! **El teléfono.**

Juan — *Repita*: el teléfono.

Repita después de Pedro.

¿Diga? – Hello?
Diga – Go ahead; I'm listening. Literally: Say. Imperative of the verb **decir** – to say; 3rd-person singular, for the polite **you.**

Pedro — ¡Es el teléfono!
¿**Diga**?
¿Diga?
…

	¿**María**?
	¡Ah, sí! ¡María!
	…
	Sí, sí. Un minuto, por favor.
	Un minuto.
	…
	¡Señor! ¡**Señor profesor**! ¡Sr. García!
	¡El teléfono! Es **la señorita María.**
Sr. García	¡Ah!
	…
	¿Diga?
(María	................)
Sr. García	¡Ah, María! Sí.
(María	................)
Sr. García	¿**Cómo**?
(María	................)
Sr. García	¿Cómo?
	María, un minuto por favor.
	¡Pedro! Pedro, por favor, ¡**la ventana!**
	¡**Cierre** la ventana!
Pedro	– Sí, señor.
	…
Sr. García	¡Uf! Gracias, Pedro.
	Ahora sí, María. Diga.
(María	................)
Sr. García	**A las nueve.**
(María	................)
Sr. García	¿No? ¿A las nueve no?
(María	................)
Sr. García	¡Ah! … **Entonces … ¿A qué hora**?
(María	................)
Sr. García	¿A qué hora?
(María	................)
Sr. García	¿A las diez?
(María	................)
Sr. García	Bien. Bien, María. A las diez.
	… A las nueve, no. ¡A las diez!
Pedro	… "A las nueve, no. ¡A las diez!"

Un minuto, por favor. – Just a minute, please.

¿Cómo? – What did you say? (How's that?)

¡Cierre la ventana! – Close the window!
cierre – close. Imperative of the verb **cerrar**; 3rd-person singular, for the polite **you**. Notice the change in the root vowel.
Ahora sí. – That's better.
a las nueve – at nine o'clock

entonces – then
¿A qué hora? – What time? At what time?
The interrogative **qué** has a written accent to distinguish it from **que,** which means who, whom, that, and which when used as relative pronouns.

Juan	Bueno, bueno.
	Ahora, *repita*: **María viene** a las diez.
	María no viene a las nueve.
	Conteste: ¿**Viene María** a las ocho?
	– No, María no viene …
Juanita	– No, María no viene a las ocho.
Juan	*Conteste*: ¿Viene María a las siete? – No, …
Juanita	– No, María no viene a las siete.
Juan	¿Viene a las seis? – No, …
Juanita	– No, no viene a las seis.
Juan	Entonces, ¿a qué hora viene María?
Juanita	– María viene a las diez.
Juan	Sí. **Viene** a las diez.
	¿Y Pedro?
(Pedro	Buenos días, Sr. García; son las nueve.)
Juan	¿Viene Pedro a las diez? – No, Pedro no viene …
Juanita	– No, Pedro no viene a las diez.
Juan	¿A qué hora viene Pedro?
Juanita	– Pedro viene a las nueve.
	– Viene a las nueve.
Juan	¿Son las ocho ahora? – No, ahora no son …

María viene – María's coming. From the verb **venir.** Notice the change in the root vowel (as in **cierre**).
No viene. – She's not coming.
You say **no** in Spanish the same way as in English.

Viene (a las nueve). – He's coming (at nine). Notice that the subjective personal pronoun is often omitted. **Él viene** is emphatic, as in "He's the one who's coming."

Juanita – No, ahora no son las ocho.

Juan ¿Son las siete ahora? – No, ahora …

Juanita – No, ahora no son las siete.

– Ahora son las nueve y quince minutos.

…

Juan ¿Y ahora?

Juanita – Las nueve y **dieciséis** minutos,

…

diecisiete,

dieciocho,

diecinueve,

veinte.

…

Las nueve y veinte.

Juan Entonces, … ¿qué hora es?

Juanita – Son las nueve y veinte.

Juan Y ahora, por favor, *repita* **los números***:*

veinte,

diecinueve,

dieciocho,

diecisiete,

No, ahora no son las ocho. – No, it isn't eight o'clock now.

¿Y ahora? – And now?

Numbers from 16 to 20: **dieciséis, diecisiete, dieciocho, diecinueve, veinte.**

Son las nueve y veinte. – It's nine-twenty.
Repita los números. – Repeat the numbers.
número – The stress doesn't fall where you expect it to, so there's a written accent. (The same is true of **teléfono, música, japonés, después.**)

dieciséis,

quince,

catorce,

trece,

doce,

once,

diez.

Muy bien … y … muchas gracias.

muy bien – very good, very well
y muchas gracias – and thanks a lot

•••

FIN DE LA **ESCENA 2**

Exercise 2

1. Write.

4: ____________	7: ____________	2: ____________
8: ____________	3: ____________	9: ____________
5: ____________	6: ____________	1: ____________

2. ¿Cuántos son tres y dos?

3. ¿Cuántos son cinco y cuatro?

4. Read in Spanish: 10 + 2 = 12
7 + 4 = ?

5. Yes or no (True or false)

	Sí	No
Seis y cinco son once.	☐	☐
Una peseta y dos pesetas son cinco pesetas.	☐	☐
Cuatro y cuatro no son ocho.	☐	☐
El Chevrolet es un coche americano.	☐	☐
El Toyota es un coche japonés.	☐	☐
El Peugeot es un coche francés.	☐	☐

CORRECCIÓN.

1. Cuatro, ocho, cinco, siete, tres, seis, dos, nueve, uno.
2. Tres y dos son cinco.
3. Cinco y cuatro son nueve.
4. Diez y dos son doce.
   ¿Cuántos son siete y cuatro?
   (Siete y cuatro son once)
5. Sí, No, No, Sí, Sí, Sí.

ESCENA 3

VOCABULARIO BÁSICO — Basic Vocabulary

Juan	¡Shhh! *Escuche*:	
	...	
	el viento.	**el viento** – the wind
	Es el viento.	**Es el viento.** – It's the wind.
	Repita: esto es el viento.	**esto es** – this is, it's
	Y esto:	**y esto** – and this
	...	

es una ventana.

Repita: esto es una ventana.

Y esto:

…

Es una puerta. – It's a door.

es **una puerta.**

Repita: el viento,

la ventana,

la puerta.

Y esto:

…

¿Es una ventana? – No, no es …

Juanita – No, no es una ventana.

¿Es un reloj? – Is this a watch? The word order doesn't change in a question. Only the intonation indicates that a question is being asked.
el reloj de María – María's watch

Juan ¿Es **un reloj**?

Juanita – Sí, es un reloj.

Juan ¿Es **el reloj de María**? – No, …

Juanita – No, no es el reloj de María.

Repita: Es el reloj de Pedro.

Juan Y ahora, esto:

…

¿Es esto un reloj?

Juanita – No, no es un reloj.

Juan	**¿Qué es esto**?	**¿Qué es esto?** – What's this? **Qué** is a pronoun meaning what at the beginning of a question.
Juanita	– Es un teléfono.	
Juan	*Conteste*: ¿Es el teléfono de Pedro … o …	
	el teléfono del Sr. García?	**del Sr. García** – Mr. García's **del** = **de** + **el**
Juanita	– Es **el teléfono del Sr. García.**	
Juan	¿Y esto? … ¿Qué es? …	**¿Y esto?** – And this? **¿Qué es?** – What is it? **Es** by itself can mean it is; the subjective pronoun doesn't need to be expressed. **o** – or **una radio** – a radio (usually feminine in Spanish)
	¿Un teléfono … o … **una radio**?	
Juanita	– Es una radio.	
Juan	¡Perdón! ¿Qué es? ¿La radio … o …	
	la televisión?	**la televisión** – the television
Juanita	– Es la radio.	
Juan	¡Ya!	
	Repita: **un** teléfono … o … **el** teléfono.	
	Una radio … o … **la** radio.	
	Un reloj … o … el reloj.	
	Una puerta … o … la puerta.	
Pedro	– Un dólar americano, …	**un dólar** – one dollar
Sr. García	Dos **dólares americanos**.	**dos dólares** – two dollars. Notice the plural form **-es** for nouns ending in a consonant. Nouns and adjectives ending in a vowel take only **-s,** as in **americanos.**
Pedro	– Dos dólares americanos, tres dólares americanos, cuatro dólares americanos, cinco dólares américanos, seis dólares americanos, …	

¡Basta! – That's enough!
From the verb **bastar** – to suffice.
¡Basta ya! – That's enough now!

Sr. García: Bueno bueno, Pedro … ¡**Basta**!

¡**Basta ya**!

Pedro: Uno y uno son dos,

dos y dos son cuatro,

tres y tres son …

Sr. García: ¡Pedro, basta! ¡Ay!

Esto es … – This is …

Pedro: … Esto es la puerta …

y eso … – and that …
Esto (this) and **eso** (that) are invariable neuter pronouns: neither masculine nor feminine.

y … **eso:** …

eso es la ventana.

… Esto es un coche

y eso: …

una motocicleta – a motorcycle

es una **motocicleta.**

Sí. Eso es una motocicleta.

Esto es un perro. – This is a dog.

Esto es **un perro:** …

y eso: …

Eso es un gato. – That is a cat.

eso es **un gato.**

Esto … y … eso

Esto … y … eso

aquello – that. Spanish has three demonstrative pronouns: **éste** – this; **ése** – that; and **aquél** – that, the other. They vary according to gender and number, except for the neuter forms **esto, eso,** and **aquello,** which are invariable.

Esto … y … eso … y … eso …

y … **aquello.**

¡Ah! ¡La radio del profesor!

	¡Sr. García!	
Sr. García	¿Sí?	
Pedro	¿Qué es esto? ¿**Un piano?** ¿Es un piano?	**un piano** – a piano
Sr. García	– Sí, Pedro, es un piano.	
	…	
Pedro	¡Oh! … Y ¿eso? ¿**Qué es**? ¿Es **un violín**?	**un violín** – a violin
	¿Es un violín, no?	
Sr. García	– Sí, sí, Pedro … ¡Es un violín! ¡Ay!	
Pedro	… Y … ¿eso? Es un …	
Sr. García	– ¡Basta, Pedro!	
	Basta ya.	**Basta ya.** – That's enough now.
Pedro	Sr. García, escuche esto: …	**Escuche esto.** – Listen to this.
Sr. García	¡Ay, no, por favor!	
Juan	¡Ay, no, Pedro, por favor!	
	… ¿Qué es eso?	
Juanita	– ¿Eso? (¡Hmm!) Eso es la puerta y la ventana …	
	y un perro y un gato …	
	y dos **coches:**	**dos coches** – two cars
	un coche **grande**	**un coche grande** – a big car
	…	
	y un coche **pequeño**	**un coche pequeño** – a small car

Adjectives indicating color, shape, size, flavor, etc., usually follow the noun they modify.

...

Repita: un coche grande,

muy grande – very big

un coche **muy grande.**

Un coche pequeño,

un coche **muy pequeño.**

¿Es de María? – Is it María's?

Juan — El coche pequeño, ¿es de María?

No sé. – I don't know.
I isn't expressed. The verb ending is enough to indicate the subject.

Juanita — – ¿De María? ... **No sé.**

Juan — *Conteste*: ¿Es de María el coche pequeño?

Juanita — – No sé.

por ahora – for now

Juan — Bueno, basta **por ahora.**

Gracias.

•••

FIN DE LA **ESCENA 3**

Exercise 3

¿Qué es esto? **1.**  – Es un perro.

2.  – Es una ventana.

3.  –

4.  –

¿Qué es esto? **5.** – Es el reloj.

6.  – Es la puerta.

7.  –

8.  –

Un perro	El perro
Una ventana	La ventana

CORRECCIÓN.

3. Es una puerta.
4. Es un gato.
7. Es el teléfono.
8. Es la bicicleta.

ESCENA 4

¿QUIÉN ES USTED?

Who Are You?

Sr. García	¡Entre! ¡Sí, entre!
	...
María	Buenos días, Sr. García.
Sr. García	Buenos días, María.
Maria	**Hola**, Pedro, buenos días.
Pedro	¡Hola, María!
	¿**Cómo está**?
María	Bien, gracias. ¿Qué hora es?
Pedro	Las diez y diez, María.
María	¡Oh! ... **Lo siento.**

¿Quién? – Who? This pronoun at the beginning of a question has a written accent to distinguish it from **quien,** which means who or whom when used as a relative pronoun.
¡Entre! – Come in! Imperative of the verb **entrar;** 3rd-person singular, for the polite **you.**
Hola. – Hi. Hello.
¿Cómo está? – How are you?
está – 3rd-person singular of the verb **estar,** for the polite **you**.

Lo siento. – I'm sorry. Excuse me.

Está bien – That's all right. It's okay.
Escuela – School
española – Spanish (feminine)
¿Diga? – Hello?

¿Cómo? – What did you say? (How's that?) This adverb has a written accent to distinguish it from the conjunction **como** – as, like.

yo no soy – I'm not
yo soy – I am

español – Spanish. The letter **ñ** is pronounced like the **ni** in **onion.**

usted – you (polite)
This pronoun is used with a 3rd-person singular verb.

	Lo siento, Sr. García.
Sr. García	Bien, María. **Está bien.**
	...
María	**"Escuela** Española"
	"Escuela Española" ... ¿Diga?
	...
	¿Sí?
	...
	¿Cómo?
	...
	Un minuto por favor.
	¡Sr. García! ... ¡El teléfono!
	...
Sr. García	¿Diga?
(Un señor	... Nakamura-san ...)
Sr. García	¿Cómo?
	...
	No.
(El señor	...¿ Nakamura-san?)
Sr. García	¡No!
(El señor	...¿ Nakumura-san?)
Sr. García	¡No! **Yo no soy** el Sr. Nakamura.
	Yo soy el Sr. García: "García", no "Nakamura".
	Yo no soy el Sr. Nakamura.
(El señor	... ¿Oh? ¡Oh, perdón! Perdón ... Lo siento. Lo siento, señor.)
Sr. García	Está bien.
	...
	¡Nakamura! Yo no soy el Sr. Nakamura;
	soy el Sr. García.
	Yo no soy japonés; soy **español.**
Pedro	¡Yo soy el Sr. Nakamura!
María	Pedro, por favor ...
Pedro	¡Yo soy el Sr. Nakamura y soy japonés!
Sr. García	No, Pedro. **Usted no es japonés.**
	Usted es español.

Pedro	¿Y María?	
Sr. García	María es española.	
	María **también** es española.	**también** – also
Pedro	¿Y usted, Sr. García?	
Sr. García	Yo también.	
	Yo también soy español.	
	Soy español ... y soy profesor.	
María	¿Y usted, Pedro? ¿**Es usted** profesor?	**¿Es usted profesor?** – Are you a teacher?
Pedro	– ¿Yo? ¡Oh no, María, yo no soy profesor!	
	¡Soy **estudiante**!	
Sr. García	Sí, **usted es** estudiante.	**Usted es estudiante.** – You are a student.
Pedro	María, ¿es usted estudiante también?	
María	– No, **no soy** estudiante.	
Pedro	¿Qué es usted?	
María	– Soy **secretaria**.	**secretaria** – secretary. This word is stressed according to the rule, that is, on the next-to-last syllable (**ta**).
	Soy **la secretaria de la escuela**.	
Sr. García	Sí, María: usted es secretaria,	
	Pedro es estudiante,	
	y yo soy profesor.	
Juan	Bueno, está bien.	
	Ahora, *repita*: Yo soy – usted es.	

Yo no soy – usted no es.

Bien. ¿Y … usted?

señor, señora, señorita – sir, madam, miss
Conteste. – Answer. Imperative of the verb **contestar** – to answer; 3rd-person singular, for the polite **you.**

Sí, sí, usted – señor, señora o señorita –

ahora, conteste: ¿es usted estudiante?

– Ahora sí, soy …

Juanita – Ahora sí, soy estudiante.

estudiante de español – (a) Spanish student

Juan *Conteste*: Es usted **estudiante de español**?

– Sí, …

Juanita – Sí, soy estudiante de español.

Juan Ahora *repita esto, por favor*:

Pedro es estudiante

o: **él** es estudiante.

María es secretaria

o: **ella** es secretaria.

él – he. The personal pronoun **él** has a written accent to distinguish it from **el** – the (masculine article). Notice that you should write the accent on capital letters too.
Él es estudiante. – He is a student.
ella – she

japonés, japonesa – Japanese (masculine, feminine)

Repita: Él es español – ella es española.

Él no es japonés – ella no es japonesa.

Él – ella

español – española

japonés – japonesa

americano – americana.

Juanita *Repita*: yo soy,

usted es,

él es,

ella es.

Yo no soy,

usted no es,

él no es,

ella no es.

Muy bien. ¡**Perfecto**!

Gracias.

Let's review some forms of the verb **ser** – to be:
(yo) soy – I am
(él) es – he is
(ella) es – she is
(usted) es – you (polite) are

•••

FIN DE LA **ESCENA 4**

Exercise 4

"Soy el Sr. García"
"Soy profesor"

"Soy María"
"Soy secretaria" "

"Soy Pedro"
Soy estudiante"

Sí,	yo soy...	No,	yo no soy...
	usted es		usted no es
	él es		él no es
	ella es		ella no es

1. ¿Es usted el Sr. Rodríguez?

2. ¿Es usted la Sra. Martínez?

3. ¿Entonces, quién es usted?

CORRECCIÓN.

1. No, yo no soy el Sr. Rodríguez.
2. No, (yo) no soy la Sra. Martínez.
3. Soy el Sr. ________
   (o: la Sra. ________)
   (o: la Srta. ________)

ESCENA 5

¿CANTA USTED BIEN?

Do You Sing Well?

Juan	¡Shhh! *Escuche*: aquí está Pedro.
Pedro	Esto es un gato – **Estos** son dos **gatos**
	Eso es un perro – **Esos** son dos **perros**
	Tra la la, la la, la …
Juan	Pedro canta.
	Conteste: ¿Canta Pedro **en italiano**?
Juanita	– No, Pedro no canta en italiano.

Aquí está Pedro. – Here's Pedro.
está – is. 3rd-person form of the verb
estar – to be. The last syllable has a written accent. But the feminine demonstrative pronoun **ésta,** meaning this one, has a written accent on the first syllable.
esto – this (neuter demonstrative pronoun)
éstos – these (masculine demonstrative pronoun)
ésos – those (masculine demonstrative pronoun)
canta – sings
en italiano – in Italian

en francés – in French
en inglés – in English
una canción – a song

Juan	¿Canta Pedro **en francés**? – No, él no …
Juanita	– No, él no canta en francés.
Juan	¿Canta una canción **en inglés**?
Juanita	– No, no canta una canción en inglés.
Juan	¿Canta **en español**, ¿no? – Sí, …
Juanita	– Sí, canta en español.
Juan	¿Canta el profesor? – No, …
Juanita	– No, el profesor no canta.

¿Canta usted? – Do you sing?
No, yo no canto. – No, I don't sing.

Juan	¿Y usted? ¿Canta usted? – No, yo no …
Juanita	– No, **yo no canto.**
	– **No canto.**

entonces – then

Juan	Entonces …
(Pedro	Tra la la, la la, la)

¿Quién canta ahora? – Who's singing now?
Remember that the interrogative pronoun **¿quién?** has a written accent to distinguish it from the relative pronoun **quien,** meaning who or whom.
Verb **cantar** – to sing:
(yo) canto – I sing
(usted) canta – you (polite) sing
(él) canta – he sings
(ella) canta – she sings

Juan	¿Quién canta ahora?
Juanita	– Ahora canta Pedro.
Juan	*Repita*: yo canto,
	usted canta,
	él canta,
	ella canta.
	Escuche a Pedro:
Pedro	Uno – dos – tres – cuatro – cinco – seis –

siete – ocho – nueve – diez – once – doce …

¡María!

María – ¿Sí?

Pedro ¿Cuántos son doce y uno?

María – Trece.

Pedro ¿Cuántos?

María – Trece, Pedro, trece.

Pedro ¡Ah, sí, trece! Gracias, María. Gracias.

Gracias. – Thank you.

María – **De nada.**

De nada. – You're welcome.

De nada.

Pedro	Entonces: diez – once – doce – trece – catorce – quince – dieciséis – diecisiete – dieciocho – diecinueve – veinte …

¡María!

María – ¿Sí?

Pedro Y … ¿ **después de** veinte?

después de veinte – after twenty

María – Después de veinte, **veintiuno**.

Pedro ¡Ah, sí! Después de veinte, veintiuno.

	Gracias, María.
María	– De nada.
Pedro	Y después de veintiuno, ¿**veintidós**?
María	– Sí, claro, veintidós.

Numbers from 20 to 25: **veinte, veintiuno, veintidós, veintitrés, veinticuatro, veinticinco**

Pedro	Sí, claro, veintidós – **veintitrés** – **veinticuatro – veinticinco.**

Sí, claro. – Yes, of course.

Juan	Pedro **cuenta.**
	Él cuenta.
Pedro	¡María, María, escuche! Yo cuento en español:
	veintiséis – vientisiete – veintiocho – veintinueve
	… ¡María!
María	– Sí, Pedro: después de veintinueve, **treinta**.
Pedro	¡Ah¡ Entonces, después de treinta, **treinta y uno –**
	treinta y dos – treinta y tres – treinta y cuatro …
Juan	¡Pedro cuenta … y cuenta … y cuenta!
María	– Yo también **cuento** en español.
	Pedro, escuche: Diez

Pedro cuenta. – Pedro is counting.

Cuento. – I'm counting.

	Veinte	
	Treinta	
	Cuarenta	
	Cincuenta.	
Pedro	… **Cuarenta y ocho – cuarenta y nueve –**	
	cincuenta. Yo cuento **de** uno **a** cincuenta.	Numbers from 26 to 50. **de … a …** – from … to …
María	– ¡Y cuenta muy bien!	
Juan	Ahora, *conteste:* ¿Cuenta Pedro de uno a cincuenta? –	
	Sí, …	
Juanita	– Sí, Pedro cuenta de uno a cincuenta.	
Juan	¿Cuenta bien?	
Juanita	– Sí, cuenta bien.	
Juan	Pero usted, ¿cuenta usted ahora? – No, yo no …	
Juanita	– No, yo no cuento ahora.	
	– Ahora **no cuento**.	
Juan	¡Por favor, **cuente**! ¡Cuente … de uno … a cinco! –	**¡Cuente!** – Count! Imperative of the verb **contar;** 3rd-person singular, for the polite **you.**
	Uno, …	
Juanita	– Uno, dos, tres, cuatro, cinco.	
Juan	Perfecto. *Repita*: yo cuento,	
	usted cuenta,	
	él cuenta,	

ella cuenta.

¡Cuente usted! – You count!

Y … por favor, ¡cuente usted!

Juanita Diez – veinte – treinta – cuarenta – cincuenta (*Repita*).

Juan Repita los números: cinco – quince – cincuenta.

Juanita Y repita también estos números: cuatro – catorce – cuarenta.

Juan Y esos: tres – trece – treinta.

excelente – excellent

Juanita ¡Excelente!

entonces – then
Conteste. – Answer.

Juan Conteste, entonces: cuarenta pesos … y … cinco pesos, ¿cuántos son?

Juanita – Cuarenta pesos y cinco pesos son cuarenta y cinco pesos.

Juan ¿Y cuántas son treinta pesetas … y … veinte pesetas?

Juanita – Treinta pesetas y veinte pesetas son cincuenta pesetas.

¡Pues sí! – That's right! Well, yes!

Juan **¡Pues sí!** Exactamente.

¡Bravo! – Bravo!

¡Bravo! y gracias.

•••

FIN DE LA **ESCENA 5**

Exercise 5

1. Read in Spanish. 9, 11, 13, 15, 17, 19,
10, 12, 14, 16, 18, 20.

2. ¿Cuántos son doce y dos?

3. Read in Spanish. 13 + 3 = 16
15 + 2 = ?

4. ¿Canta el profesor?

5. ¿Es usted español?

CORRECCIÓN.

1. Nueve, once, trece, quince, diecisiete, diecinueve, diez, doce, catorce, dieciseis, dieciocho, veinte.
2. Doce y dos son catorce.
3. Trece y tres son dieciseis.
   ¿Cuántos son quince y dos? (– Son diecisiete)
4. No, el profesor no canta.
5. No, no soy español.

ESCENA 6

¿CUÁNTO DINERO TIENE USTED?

How Much Money Do You Have?

Juan	¡Shhh!
	¿Es esto música?
Juanita	– No, esto no es música.
Juan	¿Qué es, ... música ... o ... **dinero**?
Juanita	– Es dinero.

¿Es esto música? – Is this music?

¿Qué es? – What is it?
o – or
Es dinero. – It's money.

peso – Latin American monetary unit

María	Diez pesos … y cinco pesos … son … quince pesos, y cinco son veinte. Veinte pesos.

Juanita — Es **el dinero de María.**

María cuenta el dinero.

su dinero – her money

María cuenta **su dinero.**

Juan — Sí, María cuenta su dinero, pero *escuche*:

¡Silencio! – Silence!

tengo – I have. Remember the frequently used verb **tener**. **Haber,** an archaic verb meaning to have, is now used mainly as an auxiliary in conjugated verb forms.

¿Tiene usted …? – Do you have …? The verb **tener,** in the 3rd-person singular.

Pedro	Tra la la, la la, la – Tra la la, la …
María	– … veintiocho, veintinueve, treinta pesos, y diez son cuarenta … Pedro por favor, ¡shhh! ¡**Silencio**! ¡Cuento **mi dinero.** Cuarenta pesos y … seis, son cuarenta y seis pesos …
Pedro	Tra la la, la… ¿Cuarenta y seis pesos?
María	– Sí, pero …¡Shhh! Silencio. Cuarenta y siete, cuarenta y ocho, cuarenta y nueve, cincuenta. **Tengo** cincuenta pesos.
Pedro	María, … ¿**Usted … tiene …** cincuenta pesos?
María	– Sí. Yo tengo cincuenta pesos. ¿Y usted, Pedro? ¿**Tiene usted** cincuenta pesos?
Pedro	¿Yo? ¡Oh, no!
María	– ¿Cuánto dinero tiene usted, Pedro?
Pedro	Dos … o … tres pesos. Yo no sé exactamente.

	No sé exactamente.
	No sé.
María	– Pues … entonces, ¡cuente!
	¡Cuente su dinero!
Pedro	O.K.: un peso, dos … y uno, tres: tengo tres pesos.
María	– ¡Ah! ¿Trece pesos?
Pedro	¡No, **no tengo** trece pesos, tengo tres pesos!
	¡No tengo diez pesos, no tengo cinco pesos, no tengo cuatro pesos: **sólo** tengo tres pesos!
María	– ¿Sólo tres? ¡Oh! … ¡**Qué lástima**!

No sé. – I don't know. Notice again that no subjective pronoun is expressed. This is completely normal in Spanish.
pues … entonces – well, then
Cuente su dinero. – Count your money.

sólo tengo – I have only

¡Qué lástima! – What a pity!

Juan ¡Qué lástima¡ ¡Pedro sólo tiene tres pesos!

Bueno.

Ahora, *repita esto*: María cuenta su dinero.

Ella tiene cincuenta pesos.

Pedro cuenta su dinero.

Él tiene tres pesos.

Juanita *Repita*: yo tengo,

usted tiene,

él tiene,

ella tiene.

Juan Yo **no tengo**,

usted **no tiene,** él **no tiene,** ella **no tiene.**

Note: **Usted** is the polite form for **you**. The familiar form is **tú.**

Verb **tener** – to have:
(yo) tengo – I have
(usted) tiene – you have
(él) tiene – he has
(ella) tiene – she has

		Ahora *conteste:*
		…
una cassette – a cassette		¿Tiene usted una cassette? – Sí, yo …
	Juanita	– Sí, yo tengo una cassette.
	Juan	¿Tiene usted una cassette de español?
	Juanita	– Sí, tengo una cassette de español.
	Juan	¿Tiene usted cincuenta cassettes de español?
	Juanita	– No, no tengo cincuenta cassettes de español.
	Juan	¿Tiene usted el teléfono? – Sí, …
	Juanita	– Sí, tengo el teléfono.
	Juan	o: – No, …
	Juanita	– No, no tengo el teléfono.
	Juan	¿Tiene usted la radio? – Sí, …
	Juanita	– Sí, tengo la radio.
sí o no – yes or no	Juan	¿Tiene usted un coche, sí o no?
		Conteste por favor:
		....
		¡Ah! Y usted, Juanita ¿tiene usted coche?
No tengo coche. – I don't have a car. Notice that the indefinite article **un** isn't used here.	Juanita	– ¿Yo? No. Yo no tengo coche.
	Juan	¡Qué lástima!

Juanita	*Repita:* **no tengo coche.**	
	No tengo bicicleta.	
	No tengo motocicleta.	
Juan	¡Ay! ¡Qué lástima!	
	Pero usted tiene un perro, ¿no? – Sí, …	
Juanita	– Sí, tengo un perro.	
Juan	¿Uno o dos?	
Juanita	– Uno.	
	Sólo uno.	
Juan	Y … ¿gatos? ¿Tiene también gatos? – No, …	**también** – also
Juanita	– No, no tengo gatos.	**gatos** – cats
Juan	¿Tiene usted dinero? – Sí, …	
Juanita	– Sí, tengo dinero.	
	Repita: Sí, claro ¡**cómo no**!	**¡Cómo no!** – Of course!
Juan	¿Tiene usted dinero?	
Juanita	– ¡Cómo no!	
Juan	El Sr. Rockefeller tiene **mucho dinero.**	**mucho dinero** – lots of money
	Tiene mucho dinero.	
	Pedro no tiene mucho dinero.	
	Pedro tiene **poco dinero.**	**poco dinero** – not much money
	Tiene poco dinero.	

¿Y usted? ¿Tiene usted mucho dinero o poco dinero? – Yo …

¡Ya!

Y ahora, repita después de Juanita:

Possessive adjectives:
1st-person singular:
(yo): mi dinero – my money
2nd-person singular:
(tú: familiar**): tu dinero** – your money
(usted: polite**): su dinero** – your money
3rd-person singular:
(él): su dinero – his money
(ella): su dinero – her money

Juanita — Yo cuento mi dinero.

Usted cuenta su dinero.

Él cuenta su dinero.

Ella cuenta su dinero.

¡Ya está! – That's it! All done!
ya – already, now
nada – nothing

Juan — ¡**Ya está**! Gracias, Juanita.

Juanita — – De nada.

•••

FIN DE LA **ESCENA 6**

Exercise 6

1. Lea en español: 10, 20, 30, 40, 50
21, 25, 35, 39, 41

2. ¿Cuántos son treinta y quince?

3. ¿Cuántos son cuarenta y catorce?

4. ¿Tiene usted una cassette de español?

María tiene cincuenta pesos
(Es el dinero de María)

Pedro tiene tres pesos
(Es el dinero de Pedro)

Sí,	yo tengo …	No,	yo no tengo …
	usted tiene		usted no tiene
	él tiene		él no tiene
	ella tiene		ella no tiene

CORRECCIÓN.

1. Diez, viente, treinta, cuarenta, cincuenta
veintiuno, veinticinco, treinta y cinco, treinta y nueve, cuarenta y uno.
2. Treinta y quince son cuarenta y cinco.
3. Son cincuenta y cuatro.
4. Sí, tengo una cassette de español.

ESCENA 7

UNA LECCIÓN DE GEOGRAFÍA — A Geography Lesson

Carlos	¡Hola, **Teresa**!
Teresa	¡Hola, **Carlos**!
Carlos	¡Hola, **Felipe**!
Felipe	¡Hola! ¿Cómo está?
Carlos	Bien ...
Pedro	¡Shhh! Viene el profesor.
	Aquí viene.
	...
Sr. García	¡Silencio!
	¡Pedro, **siéntese**!

Aquí viene. – Here he comes.
Siéntese. – Sit down. Imperative of the verb **sentarse;** 3rd-person singular, for the polite **you.**
sentarse – to sit down. A reflexive verb. In the imperative and infinitive, the pronoun **se** can be attached to the end of the verb.

	Carlos también, ¡Siéntese por favor! ¡Siéntese!
	…
	Y ahora Pedro, ¡cuente a **los estudiantes**!
Pedro	Uno, dos, tres, cuatro, cinco estudiantes.

los – the. Plural of **el** (masculine)

Juan *Conteste*: ¿Cuenta Pedro los coches? – No, …

Juanita – No, Pedro no cuenta los coches.

Juan ¿Cuenta Pedro los gatos y los perros?

– No, …

Juanita – No, no cuenta los gatos y los perros.

Juan Felipe, Teresa y Carlos son estudiantes,

¿verdad? – Sí, son …

¿verdad? – right?
Literally: (Is it the) truth? This is the equivalent of the English tag questions **isn't it?, don't you?,** etc.
son – they are. Subjective pronouns are rarely expressed. The verb endings are different enough to make them understood.

Juanita – Sí, son estudiantes.

Repita: Felipe, Teresa y Carlos son

estudiantes también.

Son estudiantes también.

Juan *Repita*: un estudiante – estudiantes.

una secretaria – secretarias.

Juanita *Repita*: **el** estudiante – **los** estudiantes.

la secretaria – **las** secretarias.

las – the. Plural of **la** (feminine)

Juan *Escuche*.

Sr. García	Carlos, siéntese por favor y cuente a los estudiantes, pero …
(Sra. X	**Don Miguel** es español …)
(Sra. Y	No señora, don Miguel no es español. Don Miguel es italiano…)
Sr. García	¡Pedro, por favor, cierre la puerta! ¡Cierre la puerta!

pero – but
Don Miguel – The title **don** before a masculine given name shows respect.

cierre – close. Imperative of the verb **cerrar**; 3rd-person singular, for the polite **you.**

Juan *Repita*: Pedro **va** … a la puerta.

Pedro va a la puerta.

No va a la ventana; va a la puerta.

va – he's going. From the verb **ir** – to go.

(Sra. X	Pero Don Miguel es español.)
(Sra. Y	¡**Que no**! Don Miguel es italiano.)
(Sra. X	No sé, no sé.)
Sr. García	Pedro, ¡cierre la puerta!

¡Que no! – By no means! Not at all!
no sé – I don't know. From the verb **saber** – to know.

Juan *Conteste*: ¿**Cierra Pedro** la puerta? – Sí, …

Juanita – Sí, **Pedro cierra** la puerta.

Juan ¿**No cierra** la ventana? – No, …

Juanita – No, no cierra la ventana.

Juan ¿Qué cierra?

Juanita – Cierra la puerta.

¿Qué cierra? – What's he closing?
¿Qué? – What? The interrogative form has a written accent, in contrast to the relative pronoun **que** and the conjunction **que.**

con Pedro – with Pedro	Juan	*Conteste*: ¿Está usted en la clase con Pedro?
	Juanita	– No, yo no estoy en la clase con Pedro.
		No estoy en la escuela.
		No estoy en la oficina.
en mi casa – at home, in my house		¡Estoy en **mi casa**!
usted – you. From the contraction of **vuestra merced** (your grace), so it's followed by a verb in the 3rd-person singular. Likewise, adjectives pertaining to **usted** are singular (masculine or feminine), and the possessive adjective is **su** – your.	Juan	*Conteste*: ¿Está usted en Madrid?
	Juanita	– No, no estoy en Madrid.
	Juan	¿Está usted en **Barcelona**?
	Juanita	– No, no estoy en Barcelona.
¿en qué ciudad? – in what city? The interrogative adjective **qué** is written with an accent.	Juan	¿**En qué ciudad** está usted?
¿Y en qué país está? – And what country are you in?		¡Ah! ¿Y **en qué país** está?
		....
		Muy bien. Entonces *repita*: Yo estoy,
		usted está, él está, ella está.
en su casa – at home, in your house		Ahora usted está en su casa.
		Conteste: ¿Canta usted una canción? – No, ...
	Juanita	– No, no canto una canción.
	Juan	¿Cuenta usted su dinero? – No, ...
	Juanita	– No, no cuento mi dinero.
¿Qué hace usted? – What are you doing? This is the very useful verb **hacer,** meaning to do, in the 3rd-person singular, for the polite **you.**	Juan	No canta y no cuenta... **¿Qué hace usted?**
		¿Qué hace usted? ¿Escucha?

Juanita – Sí, escucho.

Juan ¿Escucha la cassette?

Juanita – Sí, escucho la cassette.

Juan *Conteste*: ¿Es **buena** la cassette? ¿Sí o no?

....

¡Ah!

Ahora *escuche a las dos señoras:*

¿Escucha? – Are you listening? Verb in the 3rd person, for the polite **you.** As usual, the subjective pronoun isn't expressed.
Escucho. – I'm listening.

buena – good (feminine)
¿Sí o no? – Yes or no?

Sra. X	Don Miguel **es** español y **está** en España.
Sra. Y	No, no, no, Don Miguel es italiano y está en Italia.
Sra. X	¡Ah! No sé…

•••

FIN DE LA **ESCENA 7**

Exercise 7

		Sí	No
1.	Pedro es japonés.	☐	☐
2.	El Sr. García es estudiante.	☐	☐
3.	María es americana.	☐	☐
4.	Ella es secretaria.	☐	☐
5.	Barcelona es una ciudad.	☐	☐
6.	Barcelona está en España.	☐	☐
7.	Caracas está en Venezuela.	☐	☐
8.	Madrid está en Italia.	☐	☐
9.	Nueva York está en Francia.	☐	☐
10.	María está en su oficina.	☐	☐
11.	El profesor está en su coche.	☐	☐
12.	Usted está en la clase de la escuela.	☐	☐

Sí,	yo estoy…	No,	yo no estoy…
	usted está		usted no está
	él está		él no está
	ella está		ella no está

CORRECCIÓN.

1. No, no es japonés.
2. No, no es estudiante.
3. No, no es americana.
4. Sí, es secretaria.
5. Sí, es una ciudad.
6. Sí, está en España.
7. Sí, está en Venezuela.
8. No, no está en Italia.
9. No, no está en Francia.
10. Sí, está en su oficina.
11. No, no está en su coche.
12. No, no estoy en la clase de la escuela.

ESCENA 8

LA SEÑORITA MARÍA

Miss María

Juan *No repita.*

Son las nueve. María va a la oficina **en taxi.**

María – ¡Taxi! ... ¡Taxi! ...
Avenida Central, por favor.

No repita. – Don't repeat. Negative imperative of **repetir.**

en taxi – by taxi. As in English, the 1st syllable of the word **taxi** is stressed.

Avenida Central – Central Avenue. Notice that adjectives ending in **-al** don't change when they modify a feminine noun.

Juan	*Conteste*:¿Qué es esto, un taxi o una bicicleta?
Juanita	– Es un taxi.
Juan	Muy bien. **Usted contesta** muy bien.

Contesto. – I answer. I'm answering.

Yo contesto al profesor.

La secretaria contesta el teléfono.

Ella contesta, él contesta, usted contesta.

Ahora, escuche. No repita.

María	– ¿Es **ésta** la Avenida Central?
El taxista	– Sí, señorita. Ésta es la Avenida Central. Aquí **estamos.**
María	– Gracias. ¿**Cuánto es**?
El taxista	– Son tres pesos.
María	– Tres pesos, y esto es para usted.
El taxista	– Muchas gracias, señorita.
María	– Adiós.
María	– Buenos días, Sr. López.
Sr. López	– Buenos días, María.

¿Es ésta la Avenida Central? – Is this Central Avenue?
In English we sometimes use a rising intonation to show a question, but much less often than in Spanish. Be sure to notice the written accent on the first syllable of the demonstrative pronoun **ésta.**
Aquí estamos. – Here we are. 1st-person plural of **estar.** The pronoun **nosotros, nosotras** – we (masculine, feminine) – is not expressed.
¿Cuánto es? – How much is it?
Y esto es para usted. – And this is for you. (María is giving a tip to the taxi driver.)
Muchas gracias. – Thanks a lot.
Adiós. – Good-bye.
Conteste. – Answer. Imperative of the verb **contestar** (which has nothing to do with a contest).
Aquí viene el señor López. – Here comes Mr. López.

Juan	*Conteste*: ¿Está María en **el taxi**?
Juanita	– No, María no está en el taxi.
Juan	María está en la **oficina.**
	Escuche. **Aquí** viene el Sr. López.

Sr. López	– Buenos días, María.

Juan	¿Está el Sr. López en la oficina?
Juanita	– Sí, el Sr. López está en la oficina.
Juan	¿**Está usted** en la oficina de María?
	– No, **yo no estoy ...**
Juanita	– No, yo no estoy en la oficina de María.
	– No, yo no estoy en la oficina de María.
Juan	*Repita*: Yo no estoy en su oficina.
	Escuche. *No repita*.

Una mujer	– ¿Quién es el director de la oficina?
Un hombre	– Es el Sr. López.
La mujer	– ¿Y quién es el profesor?
El hombre	– El Sr. García.
La mujer	–¡Ah!

¿Quién es el director? – Who is the (office) manager?

Juan	*Conteste*: ¿Quién es el profesor?
	¿El Sr. López o el Sr. García?
Juanita	– El profesor es el Sr. García.
Juan	¿Quién es el director de la oficina?

Juanita	– El director de la oficina es el Sr. López.
Juan	¿Quién es la secretaria?
Juanita	– La secretaria es María.
Juan	… Y el estudiante es Pedro.
	Escuche. No repita.
	Ahora Pedro no está aquí.

¿No está? – Isn't he in? The verb **estar,** used alone, can mean to be in. Notice that the subjective pronoun (**he**) is omitted.
¿Dónde está? – Where is he?

Juanita	– ¿No está?
Juan	– No, no está.
Juanita	– ¿Dónde está?
Juan	– No sé.

•••

FIN DE LA **ESCENA 8**

Exercise 8

1. Study these regular verbs: **.....AR, ...ER, ...IR**

INFINITIVO:	**CANTAR**	**COMPRENDER**	**ABRIR**	(= contrario de "cerrar")
	yo canto	yo comprendo	yo abro	
	él canta	él comprende	él abre	
	ella canta	ella comprende	ella abre	
	usted canta	usted comprende	usted abre	

Nota: yo canto = canto; yo abro = abro; yo comprendo; = comprendo; etc…

Examples of regular verbs in the infinitive:

.....AR: cantar, conjugar, contestar, entrar, escuchar, estudiar, explicar, hablar, ocupar, pasar, terminar, visitar.

.....ER: comprender, aprender, prometer, vender.

.....IR: abrir, asistir, decidir, describir, dividir, escribir, repetir.

2. Write the answers.

1. ¿Conjugo yo los verbos? – Sí, usted ______
2. ¿Canta usted bien? – Sí, (yo) ______
3. ¿Estudio yo el inglés? – No, usted no ______
4. ¿Comprende usted la lección? – Sí, (yo) ______
5. ¿Abro yo la ventana? – No, usted no ______

CORRECCIÓN.

1 – Sí, *usted conjuga* los verbos.
2 – Sí, *canto* bien (Omisión frecuente del sujeto)
3 – No, *usted no estudia* el inglés.
4 – Sí, *comprendo* la lección.
5 – No, *usted no abre* la ventana.

ESCENA 9

PEDRO ES UN ADULTO

Pedro Is An Adult

Escuche a Pedro y a María. *No repita.*

María	– ¿Pedro? ¿Es usted?
Pedro	– ¡Claro, María! ¡Soy yo!
María	– ¡Ay, cómo pasa el tiempo! Usted ya no es un niño. Ahora, usted es un adulto. Ya no es "Pedro": ahora, es "señor Pedro" o "señor don Pedro".

¡Claro! – Certainly! You bet!
¡Soy yo! – It's me all right!
soy – I am. From the verb **ser** – to be. We already know **es** – he is.

¡Ay! – Oh! This interjection often expresses regret.
¡Cómo pasa el tiempo! – How time flies!
Usted ya no es un niño. – You're not a child anymore.
ya no – not anymore, no longer

Soy una persona adulta – I'm an adult.

Pedro	– Sí, soy una persona adulta … pero también soy estudiante. Soy adulto y estudiante. El señor García es mi profesor. Él tiene muchos estudiantes adultos.
María	– ¡Oh, sí! Muchos señores y muchas señoras **estudian** con el profesor García.

muchos señores – many men, a lot of men

estudian – they're studying. From **estudiar.**

This is the first time we've seen a verb in the 3rd-person plural.

Juan ¿Quién es el estudiante?

Juanita – El estudiante es Pedro.

Juan **Pedro escribe**.

María escribe a máquina.

María escribe a máquina. – Maria's typing (using a typewriter). From **escribir.**

Conteste: ¿Es de Pedro o de María la máquina?

Juanita – La máquina es de María. *Repita*.

– La máquina es de María.

Juan ¿Quién escribe a máquina? ¿Pedro o María?

Juanita – María escribe a máquina.

Juan *Escuche*. *No repita*.

Hablan el director y la secretaria.

hablan – they're talking. 3rd-person plural of **hablar.**

Sr. López	– ¡María!
María	– Sí, Sr. López.

Sr. López	– ¿Está usted **ocupada**?
María	– ¡Sí, señor: escribo la carta para el Sr. Johnson!
Sr. López	– ¡Ah, sí! ¡La carta para el Sr. Johnson! Muy bien.

Juan *Conteste*: ¿Escribe María **una carta**?

Juanita – Sí, escribe una carta.

Juan ¿Escribe el Sr. López la carta?

Juanita – No, el Sr. López no escribe la carta.

Juan ¿Quién escribe la carta? ¿Pedro, el Sr. García, el Sr. López o María?

Juanita – María escribe la carta.

Juan ¿Es una carta para usted o para el Sr. Johnson?

Juanita – Es una carta para el Sr. Johnson.

Juan Ahora viene el profesor, el Sr. García.

Escuche. No repita.

Hablan el Sr. García y María:

ocupada – busy (feminine). Another example of that wonderfully simple Spanish spelling: just one **c.**

escribo – I'm writing

para – for. Between them, **para** and **por** take care of various meanings of the English word **for.** In this case, as it often does, **para** expresses destination. Used with a verb, it usually expresses purpose.

muy bien – fine

la carta – the letter. This word doesn't mean cart!

¡Claro que sí! – Of course!
siempre – always
escribo – I write. From the verb **escribir.**

Sr. García	– Hola, María.
María	– Hola, Sr. García.
Sr. García	– María, **¿cómo** escribe usted **las cartas**? ¿A máquina?
María	– ¡**Claro que sí**! ¡A máquina! En la oficina **siempre** escribo a máquina.

Juan ¿Cómo escribe María?

Juanita – Escribe a máquina.

¿Diga? – Hello? Literally: Say?

María	¿Diga?

Juan ¿Quién contesta el teléfono?

Juanita – María contesta el teléfono.

Sr. López	– ¡María, por favor!
María	– Sí, Sr. López.

Juan ¿Quién contesta **al** Sr. López?

Juanita – María contesta al Sr. López.

Juan *Escuche* **al** Sr. López, y **a** María.

No repita.

Escuche al señor López. – Listen to Mr. López.
al = **a** + **el**. Notice the **a** before the object: **escuchar a alguien** – to listen to someone. Here's a rule: when the object of a verb is a person or a personified living being, it's preceded by the preposition **a,** even when **to** wouldn't be used in English. Ex.: **Quiero a mi hija** – I love my daughter.
El señor Johnson habla español. – Mr. Johnson speaks Spanish.
Lo habla muy bien. – He speaks it very well.
lo – it. Objective pronoun.

Sr. López	– María, ¿escribe usted la carta para el Sr. Johnson **en** español o **en** inglés?
María	– En español. Escribo la carta en español: el Sr. Johnson habla español. **Lo** habla muy bien.
Sr. López	– ¡Ah, sí! Él habla español.

Juan ¿En qué idioma escribe María?

Juanita – María escribe en español.

¿en qué idioma? – in what language? As you can see, **qué,** meaning what or which, can be an adjective as well as a pronoun. Here it's used in a question.

Juan ¿Habla español el Sr. Johnson?

Juanita – Sí, el Sr. Johnson habla español.

Juan ¿Está el Sr. Johnson en la oficina?

Juanita – No, el Sr. Johnson no está en la oficina.

Juan ¿Están María y el Sr. López en la oficina?

Juanita – Sí, María y el Sr. López están

en la oficina.

– Sí, María y el Sr. López están en la

oficina.

Juan *Repita*: ellos están, yo estoy, él está, ella está, usted

ellos están – they (masculine) are

está.

Conteste: ¿Está usted en la oficina de María?

Juanita – No, yo no estoy en la oficina de María.

– No, yo no estoy.

¿Dónde está usted? – Where are you?
¿en la casa? – in your house? at home?

Juan ¿Dónde está usted? ¿En la casa?

– Sí, estoy …

Juanita – Sí, estoy en la casa.

Juan *Repita*: yo estoy **en mi casa.**

Él está **en su casa;**

Ella está en su casa. – She's at home.

ella está **en su casa.**

•••

FIN DE LA **ESCENA 9**

Exercise 9

Study these irregular verbs.

SER:	yo	soy	**ESTAR:**	yo	estoy
	él	es		él	está
	ella	es		ella	está
	usted	es		usted	está
	ellos	son		ellos	están
	ellas	son		ellas	están
	ustedes	son		ustedes	están

The verb SER shows:

1.	Ownership	:	La máquina es de María.
2.	Origin	:	El Sr. Johnson es de Nueva York.
3.	Nationality	:	El Sr. Tihuacán es mejicano.
4.	Profession	:	Yo soy profesor.
5.	A characteristic	:	América es muy grande.
6.	The time or day	:	Ahora son las ocho.

The verb ESTAR shows:

1.	A location	:	Madrid está en España. ¿Dónde está Pedro?
2.	A temporary condition	:	Estoy en mi casa. ¿Cómo está usted?

Be careful not to confuse the verb ESTAR

(a) with the demonstrative adjectives (este…., esta…., estos…., estas….)

Ejemplos: este señor es mejicano, esta señora es mejicana,
estos señores son mejicanos, estas señoras son mejicanas.

b) with the demonstrative pronouns (éste, ésta, éstos, éstas)

Ejemplos: éste es mejicano, ésta es mejicana,
éstos son mejicanos, éstas son mejicanas.

ESCENA 10

CONVERSACIONES EN LA OFICINA

Conversations in the Office

conversaciones – conversations. **-es** is the plural form of **conversación,** which ends in a consonant.

Juan *Escuche* al director y a la secretaria.

No repita.

Sr. López	– María, por favor, **venga** aquí.
María	– Sí, Sr. López.
Sr. López	– Venga aquí con la carta para el Sr. Johnson.

venga – come. Imperative of the verb **venir** – to come; 3rd-person singular, for the polite **you.**

voy – I'm going. 1st-person singular of the verb **ir** – to go.
en seguida – right away

María	– Sí, Sr. López. **Voy en seguida. En seguida.**

ha terminado – (she) has finished. This is the first verb we've seen in the present perfect tense.
As in English, the present perfect is formed with an auxiliary (a form of **haber** – to have) and the past participle. The form of the past participle doesn't change, so you don't have to worry about remembering number and gender agreement.
va – she's going

¿cuándo? – when?

Juan — María **ha terminado** la carta y va en seguida.

¡No va a las seis, a las siete o a las

ocho!

¡Va ahora! Va en seguida.

¡A las seis, no! ¡A las siete, no!

¡A las ocho, no!

¿Cuándo?

Juanita — – En seguida. *Repita*: en seguida.

Two polite expressions to remember:
gracias por ... – thanks for ...
De nada. – You're welcome. (It's nothing. Don't mention it.)
fotocopia – photocopy. The English **ph** is replaced by **f.** So is the **ph** in **orthography: ortografía.**

Sr. López	– ¡Gracias **por** la carta, María!
María	– De nada, señor. Ésta es **la fotocopia.**

Juan — *Repita*: ¡Gracias por la carta!

¡Gracias por la fotocopia!

Sr. López	– Y esto es para **la computadora.**
María	– Bien.

la computadora – the computer

Juan *Repita*: la computadora.

Juan Ahora *escuche* **otra vez** al profesor y a María. *No repita*.

Escuche otra vez. – Listen again. (Listen one more time.)

Sr. García	– María, ¿está aquí mi estudiante?
María	– ¿Su estudiante?
Sr. García	– Sí, sí, Pedro Aragón, mi estudiante. ¿Está con usted?
María	– No, Sr. García. Pedro no está aquí.
Sr. García	– ¿**Que** no está? ¿Pero dónde está?
María	– No sé, pero aquí no está.
Sr. García	– ¡Caramba! **Tengo cita** con mi estudiante y no está aquí!
María	– ¡No, no está aquí!

su estudiante – your student
su – your. The 3rd-person possessive adjective is used here to correspond to **usted.**
con usted – with you (polite singular)
¿Que no está? Que sometimes means **porque** – because. In this case, it expresses indignation. "What do you mean, he isn't here!" cried Mr. García before uttering his only swearword of the whole course.
¡Caramba! – Good grief!

Juan ¿Está Pedro en la oficina?

Juanita – No, Pedro no está en la oficina.

Juan Repita **la forma negativa** del **verbo:** Él no está, ella no está, usted no está, ellos no están.

Ellos no están. – They're not here. They're not in (the office).

los Sres. = abbreviation of **los señores.** Though more common, the equivalent of **Messrs** (from the French **messieurs)** used as the plural of **Mr. Fulano y Mengano** are used here as generic surnames (**apellidos**). Remember that, like most words ending in a vowel, they're stressed on the next-to-last syllable.

las Sras. = abbreviation of **las señoras.** Though more common, the equivalent of **Mmes** (from the French **mesdames)** used as the plural of **Mrs.** (or **madame, madam**).

ellas – they (feminine). A subjective pronoun, not always expressed.

	Conteste: ¿Están **los Sres.** Fulano y Mengano en la oficina?
	– No, **ellos no están...**
Juanita	– No, ellos no están en la oficina.
Juan	¿Están **las Sras.** Carmen y Teresa en la oficina?
	– No, **ellas** no están ...
Juanita	– No, ellas no están en la oficina.
Juan	*Repita*: ellos – ellas.
Juan	*Escuche. No repita*.

¿Qué pasa? – What's happening?
Lo siento. – I'm sorry.
¿Sabe usted? – Do you know? From the verb **saber** – to know.
No lo sé. – I don't know (it).
Llaman. – Literally: They're calling. Indefinite 3rd-person plural, which can mean either they or somebody, as in "Somebody's ringing the bell" or "They're knocking at the door."
Abra – Open. Imperative of **abrir;** the polite **you.**
¡Aquí estoy! – Here I am!
¡Por fin! – At last!
Mi reloj se ha parado. – My watch has stopped. Present perfect tense of the reflexive verb **pararse** – to stop.

Sr. García	– ¡Sr. López!
Sr. López	– ¿Sí? ¿**Qué pasa**?
Sr. García	– ¿Dónde está Pedro?
Sr. López	– ¿Pedro?
Sr. García	– Sí, Pedro Aragón, mi estudiante. ¿No está en su oficina?
Sr. López	– No, en mi oficina no está. **Lo siento.**
Sr. García	– ¿**Sabe usted** dónde está?
Sr. López	– No, no **lo** sé. ¡Ah! ¡**Llaman** a la puerta! ¡María! ... **Abra** la puerta, por favor.
María	– Sí, **voy** en seguida ...
Pedro	– ¡Buenos días! ¡**Aquí estoy**!
Sr. García	– ¡**Por fin**!
Pedro	– Lo siento, Sr. García. **Mi reloj se ha parado.**

Juan — Ahora, el Sr. López, María, el Sr. García y Pedro están **juntos.**

Ellos están juntos.

Están **todos juntos.**

El Sr. López, María, el Sr. García, Pedro …

¡todos! *Repita*: todos.

Esto es **una recapitulación.**

Repita: él está en su oficina,

ella está en su oficina,

usted está en su oficina,

yo estoy en mi oficina.

Repita: usted y yo.

Usted y yo **estamos** …

en **nuestras oficinas.**

Repita otra vez: estamos en nuestras oficinas.

Juan — ¡Y la escena **ha terminado**!

Juanita — ¡Adiós!

juntos – together (masculine plural). Literally: joined.

todos – all. Indefinite pronoun. **todo, toda** (masculine and feminine singular); **todos, todas** (masculine and feminine plural).

usted y yo estamos – you and I are
en nuestras oficinas – in our offices

Possessive adjectives:
mi – my
su – your (corresponding to **usted**)
su – his, her
nuestras – our
ha terminado – has ended, is finished

•••

FIN DE LA **ESCENA 10**

Exercise 10

1. Study these two irregular verbs.

IR:	yo	voy	**VENIR:**	yo	vengo
	él	va		él	viene
	ella	va		ella	viene
	usted	va		usted	viene
	ellos	van		ellos	vienen
	ellas	van		ellas	vienen
	ustedes	van		ustedes	vienen

EJEMPLOS: ¿Adónde va el avión? – El avión va a Tokio.
¿De dónde viene el avión? – El avión viene de Nueva York.

2. Possessive adjectives
Note: *Su* can mean his, her, your, or their.

	Singular	**Plural**
(yo)	MI, MI,	MIS, MIS
(él, ella, usted)	SU, SU,	SUS, SUS
(nosotros, nosotras)	NUESTRO, NUESTRA,	NUESTROS, NUESTRAS
(ellos, ellas, ustedes)	SU, SU,	SUS, SUS

Yo estoy en mi coche; yo estoy en mi casa; yo escucho mis cassettes.
Él está en su coche; él está en su casa; él escucha sus cassettes (plur.).
Ella está en su coche; ella está en su casa; ella escucha sus cassettes.
Ud. está en su coche; Ud. está en su casa; Ud. escucha sus cassettes.

Nosotros (o nosotras) estamos en nuestro coche
("coche", masculino singular ⟶ "nuestro", masculino singular).
estamos en nuestra casa
("casa", femenino singular ⟶ "nuestra", femenino singular).
estamos en nuestros coches (masculino plural).
estamos en nuestras casas (femenino plural).
Ellos (ellas, ustedes) están en su coche o en su casa, y escuchan sus discos y sus cassettes.

ESCENA 11

POSICIONES Y SITUACIONES

Positions and Situations

Juan *Escuche. No repita.*

Sr. García	– ¡Pedro!
Pedro	– ¿Sí, Sr. García?
Sr. García	– ¿Está **preparado**?
Pedro	– Sí, señor.
Sr. García	– Bien. ¿Tiene usted su **bolígrafo**?
Pedro	– Sí, sí, aquí **lo** tengo.
Sr. García	– Bien. ¡Entonces, para **comenzar, un ejercicio! Escriba** esto:

¿Está preparado? – Are you ready?
¿Tiene su bolígrafo? – Do you have your (ballpoint) pen?
Aquí lo tengo. – I have it (here).

para comenzar – to start with
Escriba. – Write.

	"Yo estoy en mi casa" ¡Y ahora: él, ella y usted!
Pedro	– "Él está en su casa" "Ella está en su casa" "Usted está en su casa."
Sr. García	– ¡Muy bien!

Juan — *Conteste*: ¿Escribe Pedro?

Juanita — – Sí, escribe.

Juan — ¿Escribe a máquina?

Juanita — – No, no escribe a máquina.

con – with

Juan — ¿Escribe con un bolígrafo?

Juanita — – Sí, escribe con un bolígrafo.

otra vez – again (one more time)

Juan — *Escuche* otra vez al Sr. García y a Pedro.

No repita.

continúa. – continues (3rd-person singular)
nosotros estamos – we are
Nosotros is the subjective pronoun, not necessarily expressed. The feminine form is **nosotras.**
ustedes – you. This is the plural form of **usted** (polite **you**).
ustedes están – you are. **Ustedes** is followed by a verb in the 3rd-person plural, and the corresponding possessive adjective is **sus.** If you remember that **ustedes** used to mean your graces, it will be easier to understand why the verb is in the 3rd person.

Sr. García	– Continúa la recapitulación. ¡Usted y yo, **nosotros**! "Nosotros estamos en nuestras casas." ¡Y ahora, ellos, ellas y ustedes!
Pedro	– ¿Ustedes?
Sr. García	– Sí, usted, usted, y usted: "ustedes", todos.
Pedro	– ¡Ah, sí! ¡Ustedes! "Ustedes están en sus casas." "Ellos están en sus casas." "Ellas están en sus casas."

Sr. García	– ¡Perfecto!

Juan *Repita*: nosotros estamos …

en nuestras casas.

Repita: yo tengo mi bolígrafo.

Nosotros tenemos nuestros bolígrafos.

Ellos, ellas y ustedes tienen sus bolígrafos.

Ellos tienen su dinero, sus coches y sus casas.

nosotros tenemos – we have
tener – to have
tienen – they have, or you have (plural polite **you**)

Juanita – Ellos tienen su dinero, sus coches y sus casas.

Juan Ustedes están en sus casas y **hablan** español.

ustedes hablan – you're speaking (plural polite **you**)

Conteste: ¿Tienen ustedes sus cassettes?

– Sí, nosotros tenemos nuestras …

Juanita – Sí, nosotros tenemos nuestras cassettes.

Juan *Repita*: nuestr**o** coche, nuestr**a** bicicleta.

Nuestr**os** coches, nuestr**as** bicicletas.

Nuestro, nuestra, nuestros, nuestras.

nuestro, nuestra – our. A singular possessive adjective, with masculine and feminine forms.
nuestros, nuestras – our (plural)

Juan *Escuche. No repita.*

Pedro	– María, esta máquina es para **fotocopiar documentos,** ¿verdad?

fotocopiar – to photocopy. Notice the **f** in Spanish, as opposed to **ph** in English.
documentos – documents

¿verdad? – right? (tag question)

una máquina de escribir – a typewriter
una computadora – a computer
¡Así! – Like this!

con ella – with her

María	– Sí.
Pedro	– Y esto es **una computadora,** ¿verdad?
María	– Sí. Es la computadora de la oficina.
Pedro	– ¿Y usted, María? ¿Usted escribe a máquina en esta computadora?
María	– ¡Claro que sí! Escribo a máquina en la máquina de escribir, pero también en la computadora.
Pedro	– ¿Cómo escribe?
María	– ¡Así!

Juan *Conteste*: ¿Está María en su casa o en la oficina?

Juanita – Está en la oficina.

Juan ¿Está Pedro **con ella**?

Juanita – Sí, Pedro está con ella. *Repita.*

Juan ¿Canta María en la oficina?

Juanita – ¡No, María no canta en la oficina!

Juan ¿Escucha música o escribe a máquina?

Juanita – Escribe a máquina.

Juan *Repita*: María es secretaria y tiene una máquina de escribir.

Juanita – María es secretaria y tiene una máquina de escribir.

Juan *Repita*: una máquina de escribir.

Escuche.

María	– Aquí, en la oficina, tengo una máquina de escribir y una computadora.
Pedro	– ¿Tiene usted una computadora en su casa también?
María	– No, en mi casa **no tengo computadora;** sólo tengo una máquina de escribir y el teléfono, claro.

No tengo computadora. – I don't have a computer.
sólo – only. A written accent is used to distinguish the adverb **sólo** from the adjective **solo** – alone.

Juan En su oficina, María tiene una máquina

de escribir y una computadora.

En su casa, María sólo tiene una máquina

de escribir.

sólo tiene – has only

Juan Pero tiene también teléfono, ¿verdad?

– Sí, tiene también …

pero tiene también … – but she also has …

Juanita – Sí, tiene también teléfono.

Juan ¿Tiene ella una computadora en su casa?

Juanita – No, ella no tiene computadora en su casa.

– No, no tiene computadora en su casa.

•••

FIN DE LA **ESCENA II**

Exercise 11

1. Verbs of this type: **O ⟶ UE (ejemplo: contar cuento)**

CONTAR
yo cuento
usted cuenta
él cuenta
ella cuenta
nosotros contamos
nosotras contamos
ustedes cuentan
ellos cuentan
ellas cuentan

Otros verbos del tipo O ⟶ UE:
COSTAR: El disco cuesta mil pesetas.
DEMOSTRAR: El profesor demuestra una teoría.
ENCONTRAR: Yo no encuentro mi bolígrafo. ¿Dónde está?
RESOLVER: Pedro resuelve un problema de matemáticas.

2. Verbs of this type: **E ⟶ IE:**

CERRAR ⟶ cierro
yo cierro
usted cierra
él cierra
ella cierra
nosotros cerramos
nosotras cerramos
ustedes cierran
ellos cierran
ellas cierran

PREFERIR ⟶ prefiero
yo prefiero
usted prefiere
él prefiere
ella prefiere
nosotros preferimos
nosotras preferimos
ustedes prefieren
ellos prefieren
ellas prefieren

Otros verbos del tipo E ⟶ IE:
COMENZAR: La lección 12 comienza aquí.
EMPEZAR: La lección 12 empieza aquí.
REFERIR: El estudiante se refiere al diccionario.
GOBERNAR: Este ministro gobierna su país.
DEFENDER: El soldado defiende su posición.
SENTIR: Pedro siente no saber escribir a máquina.

ESCENA 12

¡AQUÍ SE HABLA ESPAÑOL!

Spanish Is Spoken Here

La mujer	– El Sr. García es profesor de español.

Juan	Yo también soy profesor de español.
	El Sr. García y yo **somos** profesor**es.**

somos – we are

otros – others (masculine)

Pedro y **otros estudiantes** (juntos)	– ¡Pero nosotros somos estudiant**es!**

Juan	*Repit***an:** Nosotros somos estudiantes.
	*Contest***en:** ¿Son ustedes estudiantes de español o de francés?
	– Nosotros somos …
Juanita	– Nosotros somos estudiantes de español.
Juan	*Escuche.*

son – they are
Verb **ser** – to be. So far we've encountered the following forms:
soy – I am
es – he or she is
es – you (usted) are
somos – we are
son – they are
¿son ustedes?– are you? (polite plural)

Sr. García y Juan (juntos)	– Y nosotros somos profesores.
Una señorita	– ¿Profesores? ¡Ah! "Do you teach English?" ¿Son ustedes profesores **de** inglés?
Sr. García y Juan (juntos)	– No, no, no, señorita …
Sr. García	– No somos profesores de inglés; somos profesores de español. En la escuela siempre **hablamos** español.
Juan	– Y en las cassettes también, siempre hablamos español con nuestros estudiantes.

profesor – teacher, professor. The stress falls on the last syllable, as in nearly all words ending in a consonant.
profesores – teachers, professors. The usual plural form for nouns ending in a consonant is **-es.**
Do you teach English? The student asks the question in English.

siempre hablamos – we always speak

Juan Nosotros **siempre** hablamos español

con nuestros estudiantes.

Y en la oficina también, María y

el Sr. López siempre hablan español.

Escuche ahora al Sr. López y a María.

Sr. López	– ¡María!
María	– ¿Sí, señor López?
Sr. López	– ¿Ha terminado la carta para el Sr. Johnson?
María	– Sí, señor.
Sr. López	– ¿Dónde está?
María	– La carta está en la mesa, Sr. López, cerca del teléfono.

La carta está en la mesa. – The letter is on the table.
en – in, on, at
en la escuela – in (at) school
en la oficina – in (at) the office
en casa – at home
en mi casa – at home, in my house
en las cassettes – on the cassettes
en España – in Spain
en la mesa – on the table
cerca del teléfono – near the telephone
cerca de – near
busca – he's looking for
pero no encuentra – but he can't find (it)

Juan El Sr. López **busca** la carta.

Busca y busca y busca ...

pero no encuentra la carta.

Repita: El Sr. López no encuentra la carta.

María	– Delante de usted.
Sr. López	– ¿Delante de **mí?**
María	– ¡Aquí, Sr. López, con **la correspondencia**!
Sr. López	– ¡Ah! Sí. Gracias, María.

delante de – in front of
delante de mí – in front of me
aquí con la correspondencia – here, with the mail

María	– De nada, señor.

ha encontrado – has found

detrás de él – behind him
detrás de – behind

Juan *Repita*: El Sr. López **ha encontrado** la carta.

¿Dónde está la carta?

¿Delante de él o detrás de él?

Juanita – La carta está delante de él. *Repita*.

– La carta está delante de él.

Juan ¡Sí, claro! *Escuche*. *No repita*.

Aquí lo tiene. – Here it is. (Here you have it.)
papel – paper

Estimado señor – Dear Sir. Remember this salutation, which is useful for beginning a business letter or an administrative request.
contesto – I am answering
del día 4 – of the fourth
día – day (masculine)

Sr. López	– Un bolígrafo, por favor.
María	– Aquí **lo** tiene, señor.
Sr. López	– Gracias. Y **papel** para escribir, por favor.
María	– El papel está en la mesa, señor: aquí lo tiene.
Sr. López	– ¡Ah! Sí, gracias. "**Estimado** señor, **Contesto** a su carta del día 4 …

Juan *Repita*: el señor tiene un bolígrafo.

Tiene un bolígrafo y papel para escribir.

Conteste: ¿Escribe a máquina?

Juanita – No, no escribe a máquina. *Repita*.

Juan *Conteste*: ¿Escribe con un bolígrafo?

Juanita – Sí, escribe con un bolígrafo.

Juan ¿Escribe **en** el papel?

en el papel – on the paper

Juan *Escuche. No repita.*

Pedro	– El señor López escribe.
Sr. García	– ¿**En qué** escribe?
Pedro	– En un papel.
Sr. García	– ¿Con qué?
Pedro	– Con un bolígrafo.

¿En qué escribe? – What's he writing on?
¿Con qué? – With what?
Plural nouns: **papel – papeles; profesor – profesores**
Each of these words ends in a consonant, so the plural is formed by adding **-es.**
bolígrafo – bolígrafos
máquina – máquinas
The plural of words ending in a vowel is formed by adding **-s.**

Juan *Repita*: papel – papel**es**

bolígrafo – bolígrafo**s**

máquina – máquina**s**

Conteste: ¿Escribe María con un bolígrafo?

Juanita – No, ella no escribe con un bolígrafo.

Juan ¿Qué hace María?

¿Escribe a máquina?

Juanita – Sí, escribe a máquina.

Juan *Repita*: ¿Qué hace María?

¿Qué hace María? – What's María doing?

Ahora *Conteste*: ¿Qué hace Pedro?

Juanita – Pedro canta.

I speak English. Here Mr. Miller is speaking English.

Sr. Miller	– "I speak English!"

Juan	¿Qué hace el Sr. Miller?
Juanita	– Habla inglés.
Juan	¡Pero nosotros, no!
	¡Nosotros siempre hablamos español!

¡Pero nosotros, no! – But we don't! (But not us!)

•••

FIN DE LA **ESCENA 12**

Exercise 12

1. Study the present perfect tense of these regular verbs: visit, learn, decide.

VISITAR	APRENDER	DECIDIR
yo he visitado	he aprendido	he decidido
él (ella, usted) ha visitado	ha aprendido	ha decidido
nosotros (o nosotras*)hemos visitado	hemos aprendido	hemos decidido
ellos (ellas, ustedes) han visitado	han aprendido	han decidido, etc.

EJEMPLO (con el Pretérito perfecto del verbo "terminar"): Ellos han terminado el ejercicio 11, pero no han terminado el ejercicio 12.

2. Write the answers in the present perfect tense.

1. ¿Ha escuchado usted la escena 12?
   – Sí, yo ____________________
2. ¿Ha contestado (usted) bien?
   – Sí, (yo) ____________________
3. ¿Ha comprendido (usted)?
   – Sí, (yo) ____________________
4. ¿He explicado yo el vocabulario?
   – Sí, usted ____________________
5. ¿Han visitado ustedes el museo?
   – Sí, nosotros ____________________

*Note: *Nosotras* is the feminine form of *nosotros.*

CORRECCIÓN.

1 – Sí, yo *he escuchado* la escena 12.
2 – Sí, (yo) *he contestado* bien.
3 – Sí, *he comprendido.*
4 – Sí, usted *ha explicado* el vocabulario.
5 – Sí, nosotros *hemos visitado* el museo.

ESCENA 13

LAS PREGUNTAS Y LAS CONTESTACIONES

Questions and Answers

Juan *No repita.*

Sr. García	– "¿ Qué hace?" es **una pregunta**.
Pedro	– ¿ Una pregunta?
Sr. García	– Sí, una pregunta. "¿ Qué hace Ud.?", "¿Dónde está Ud.?", "¿Quién es usted?", "¿Qué hora es?", **etc.** son **preguntas.** Pedro, ¿sabe usted **las contestaciones** a las preguntas?
Pedro	– ¿Las contestaciones?

una pregunta – a question

Ud. – abbreviation of **usted**

las contestaciones – the answers. Plural **-es** ending of **contestación.**

Sr. García	– Sí, las contestaciones a las preguntas.
Pedro	– ¡Ah! Sí. Las contestaciones son: “Yo hablo español”, “Estoy en la clase de la escuela”, “Soy Pedro”, y “Ahora son las diez”. **Éstas** son las contestaciones!
Sr. García	– Muy bien, Pedro: **sus** contestacion**es** son correct**as.**

éstas – these (feminine plural). Notice that there is also a written accent on the capital letter.
correctas – correct (feminine plural)

Juan *Repita*: una pregunta y una contestación.

Repita las preguntas:

¿Qué hace usted? ¿Qué **hago** yo?

Ahora *conteste* mi pregunta:

¿Hago yo las preguntas en inglés o en español?

– Usted hace las preguntas …

Juanita – Usted hace las preguntas en español.

– Usted hace las preguntas en español.

Juan *Conteste*: ¿Hace usted los **ejercicios** del libro?

– Sí, yo hago los ejercicios …

Juanita – Sí, yo hago los ejercicios del libro. *Repita*.

– Sí, hago los ejercicios del libro.

Juan *Repita*: yo hago, usted hace,

nosotros **hacemos**, ustedes **hacen**.

Escuche **lo que** hace Pedro.

¿Qué hago yo? – What am I doing?

en inglés – in English

del libro – of (in) the book
del = **de** + **el**

hacemos – we're doing
hacen – you (polite) are doing
lo que – what (that which). Notice the neuter pronoun (**lo**).

Pedro	– "Adiós muchachos compañeros de mi vida, ..."
María	– Pedro, ¿Qué hace usted?
Pedro	– ¡Canto una canción, María! ¡Es **un tango**! ¡Un tango **argentino**! ¿No me escucha usted?
María	– ¡Sí, sí, lo escucho muy bien! ¡Demasiado bien! Pedro, por favor, **¡párese de cantar!** Tengo que escribir esta carta.
Pedro	– ¡Oh! Perdón, María.
María	– Es una carta **larga**, muy larga ...
Pedro	– ¡Pero usted escribe muy rápidamente!
María	– Es que soy secretaria, Pedro.
Pedro	– Sí, lo sé. ¡Pero cómo escribe! ¡Lo hace **tan rápidamente**!
María	– Lo hago rápidamente porque soy secretaria y tengo **mucha práctica**.

muchachos – boys
compañeros de mi vida – my lifelong buddies
un tango argentino – an Argentine tango
¿No me escucha usted? – Aren't you listening to me?
demasiado – too (excessively)
Párese de cantar. – Stop singing.
parar – to stop. The verb **pararse** (to stop) is reflexive, with the pronoun **se** added to the infinitive. 1st person: **me paro.**
larga – long (feminine). Masculine: **largo.**
muy – very
muy rápidamente – very fast
tan – so
Tengo mucha práctica. – I've had a lot of practice.

Juan *Repita*: ella escribe rápidamente ...

porque tiene mucha práctica.

Juanita – Usted habla lentamente.

Juan ¿Muy lentamente?

Juanita – Sí, muy lentamente.

Juan Muy, muy, muy lentamente:

¡**demasiado** lentamente!

Repita: muy lentamente, demasiado lentamente.

porque – because
por qué – why. Note the written accent and separation of words.
lentamente – slowly

demasiado – too (excessively)

Pedro	– ¡Uno, dos, tres, cuatro, cinco, seis, siete, ocho, nueve, diez!

¿cómo? – how? Unlike the conjunction **como** (as, like), the interrogative adverb **cómo** has a written accent on the 1st syllable.

rápido – fast (masculine). Feminine: **rápida.**
para Ud., para usted – for you (polite singular)
rápido – quickly. The masculine adjective **rápido** can be used as an adverb.

así – like this

secretario – secretary (masculine)

fantástico – extraordinary, fantastic

Juan	*Conteste*: ¿Cómo cuenta Pedro?
Juanita	– Cuenta rápidamente.
Juan	¿Muy rápidamente?
Juanita	– Sí, muy rápidamente.
Juan	¿Es demasiado **rápido** para Ud.?
Juanita	– Sí, es demasiado rápido para mí.
Juan	*Escuche***lo:**

Pedro	– ¡**Rápido**! Así: ¡1, 2, 3, 4, 5, 6, 7, 8, 9, 10!
María	– ¡Pedro!
Pedro	– ¡Ah! ¡Sí! "Pedro": P – E – D – R – O. "Pedro". ¡Soy yo!
María	– Ud. cuenta rápidamente, Pedro … pero escribe a máquina muy lentamente.
Pedro	– ¡Sí, porque yo no soy secretar**io**! No tengo mucha práctica.
María	– Escuche cómo escribo yo. "María": M – A – R – Í – A.
Pedro	– ¡Ah! ¡Eso es fantástico! ¡Escribe tan rápidamente!
Un hombre en la oficina	– ¡Esta secretaria es fantástica!

Otro hombre en la oficina	– ¡Sí, es fantástica! ¡Es **verdaderamente fantástica**!
El prim**ero**	– ¿**Cómo se llama**?
El segundo	– **Se llama** María, María Fernández.

verdaderamente – really (truly)

¿Cómo se llama? – What's her name?
Se llama María. – Her name is María.

Juan *Repita*: La secretaria se llama María.

El estudiante se llama Pedro.

Repita: Él se llama Pedro y ella

se llama María.

Pedro	– Buenos días, Sr. García.

Juan *Conteste*: ¿Cómo se llama el profesor?

Juanita – El profesor se llama García.

Juan *Escuche. No repita.*

Una estudiante	– ¡Hola! ¿Quién es Ud.?
Sr. García	– ¿Yo? Pero … ¡yo soy el profesor!
La estudiante	– ¡Oh! Perdón, señor.

¡Hola! – Hi!
pero – but
¡Oh! Perdón, señor. – Oh! Excuse me, sir.

me llamo – my name is

Mucho gusto. – Glad to meet you. (It's a pleasure.)

Sr. García	– Está bien.
La estudiante	– ¿Es Ud. el Sr. Gutiérrez?
Sr. García	– No, yo **me llamo** García. ¿Y Ud., señorita? ¿Usted, quién es? ¿Cómo se llama?
La estudiante	– Yo soy estudiante y me llamo Isabel. Isabel Ortiz.
Sr. García	– **Mucho gusto**, Srta. Ortiz.
La estudiante	– **Mucho gusto**, profesor.

Juan

Conteste: ¿Y Ud.? ¿Cómo se llama Ud.?

– Yo me llamo ...

¡Ah! Muy bien.

Ahora *repita* la pregunta: ¿Cómo se llama Ud.?

Repita: yo me llamo, usted se llama, él se llama, ella se llama.

•••

FIN DE LA **ESCENA 13**

Exercise 13

1. Irregular verbs ending in **-go** in the 1st-person singular:

HACER	TENER	TRAER	VENIR	DECIR
yo **hago**	**tengo**	**traigo**	**vengo**	**digo**
él (ella, Ud.) hace	tiene	trae	viene	dice
nosotros (nosotras) hacemos	tenemos	traemos	venimos	decimos
ellos (ellas, ustedes) hacen	tienen	traen	vienen	dicen

Ejemplo: Cuando **vengo** a la oficina, digo buenos días a la secretaria.

2. Adverbs:

exacto: exactamente
(exacta, exactos, exactas)
correcto: correctamente
(correcta, etc.)
perfecto: perfectamente
(perfecta, etc.)
típico: típicamente
claro: claramente
rápido: rápidamente
lento: lentamente
científico: científicamente
fantástico: fantásticamente
maravilloso: maravillosamente

horrible: horriblemente
probable: probablemente
terrible: terriblemente
general: generalmente
excepcional: excepcionalmente
tradicional: tradicionalmente
fácil: fácilmente
cortés: cortésmente (con cortesía)
paciente: pacientemente (con paciencia)
frecuente: frecuentemente (con frecuencia)
atento: atentamente (con atención)
EXCEPCIONES: bueno: bien
malo: mal (o: malamente)

Ejemplos: Este estudiante es maravilloso: contesta maravillosamente.
Estos estudiantes son muy atentos: escuchan muy atentamente.

3. Write the adverb that corresponds to the adjective.
¡La canción es magnífica pero Pedro no canta ____________________!

Exercise 13

CORRECCIÓN.

¡La canción es magnífica pero Pedro no canta *magníficamente*!

ESCENA 14

¿CÓMO SE LLAMA USTED?

What's Your Name?

Juan	*Escuche.*
Juanita	– ¿Cómo se llama usted?
Juan	Me llamo Juan. ¿Y usted? ¿Cómo se llama?
Juanita	– Me llamo Juanita.

Pedro	– Yo me llamo Pedro. Pedro Aragón. “Pedro” es mi **nombre**.

Juan y Juanita – Juan and Juanita (John and Jean or Joan)
Practice pronouncing the Spanish **j.**

me llamo – my name is

mi nombre – my first (given) name

mi apellido – my last name (surname)

está escrito – it's written
en mi pasaporte – in my passport
con su foto – with your photograph

Pedro	"Aragón" es mi **apellido**.
María	– Yo me llamo María Fernández. "María" es mi nombre. "Fernández" es mi apellido. Está **escrito** aquí, en mi **pasaporte**.
Pedro	– ¡Ah, sí! Aquí está … con su **foto de identidad**.

Juan — *Repita*: el nombre.

El apellido.

El apellido de María es "Fernández".

El apellido de Pedro es "Aragón".

Ahora *conteste*: Pedro, María, Jorge, Carmen, Emilio,

nombres – first names

… ¿Qué son? ¿Nombr**es** o apelli**dos**? – Son …

Juanita — – Son nombres.

Juan — *Escuche*.

alemán – German (masculine).
Feminine: **alemana.**

Pedro	– El apellido "Duval" es un apellido francés. "Donati" es un apellido italiano. "Jones" es un apellido inglés o americano. "Schmidt" es un apellido alemán.
María	– Pero usted, Pedro, tiene un apellido muy español: "Aragón" es muy español.
Pedro	– Es verdad. Y usted también María, tiene un apellido español: hay muchos

> "Fernández" en España y en **Hispanoamérica** también.

Hispanoamérica – Latin America, Spanish America

Juan *Repita*: Hispanoamérica y España.

Hispanoamericano y español.

Conteste ¿Tienen Pedro y María apellidos ingleses o **hispanos**?

– **Ellos tienen ...**

Juanita – Ellos tienen apellidos hispanos.

Juan *Repita*: Ellos son españoles y tienen apellidos españoles.

Repita **el verbo "tener":** yo tengo, usted tiene, él tiene, ella tiene,

ellos tienen, ellas tienen,

usted y usted y usted: **ustedes tienen**.

Esto es el verbo "tener".

Ahora, **el verbo "ser"**:

Yo soy español y usted, Juanita, es española.

Juanita – Sí, yo soy española y usted, Juan, es español.

Juan Él es, ella es ...

hispanoamericano – Latin American, Spanish American

tienen – they have

ustedes tienen – you (polite plural) have
Verb **tener** – to have:
tengo – I have
tiene – he or she has, or you (**usted**) have
Tener and **haber** are by no means interchangeable verbs. **Tener** expresses possession, whether literal or figurative. **Haber** is now always used as an auxiliary verb (as in the present perfect tense) or as an impersonal verb (**hay** – there is, there are).

Y ahora el verbo "estar":

Yo estoy en Méjico, Ud. está en Méjico, él está, ella

está,

ellos están, ellas están,

ustedes están.

Escuche. No repita.

cuál es – what is

Pregunte. – Ask.

Isabel Ortiz (**una estudiante**)	– El profesor se llama García, pero no sé **cuál** es su nombre: ¿Antonio García? ¿Manuel García? ¿Enrique o Emilio? … No lo sé.
Otra estudiante	– ¡**Pregunte** a la secretaria!

Juan — Ahora **la estudiante pregunta** a María:

sé que … – I know that … Notice that **I** is not expressed.

Isabel Ortiz	– Por favor, señorita. Sé que el apellido de nuestro profesor es García, pero ¿cuál es su nombre?
María	– Su nombre es Sancho. El profesor se llama Sancho García.
Isabel Ortiz	– Gracias, señorita.
María	– De nada.
Isabel Ortiz	– ¡Se llama Sancho!

La otra estudiante	– **¿De verdad**?
Isabel Ortiz	– Sí.
La otra estudiante	– ¡Ay! ¡Qué nombre!

la otra – the other (feminine)
¿De verdad? – Really?

¡Ah! ¡Qué nombre! – Wow! What a name!

Juan *Conteste*: ¿Cuál es el nombre del Sr. García?

Juanita – El nombre del Sr. García es Sancho.

Juan *Repita*: su nombre es Sancho.

Conteste: ¿Cuál es su apellido?

Juanita – Su apellido es García.

•••

FIN DE LA **ESCENA 14**

Exercise 14

1. Reflexive verbs:

LLAMARse	IRse	PONERse (por ejemplo: ponerse de pie)
yo me llamo	**me voy**	**me pongo**
usted se llama	se va	se pone
él se llama	se va	se pone
ella se llama	se va	se pone
nosotros nos llamamos	nos vamos	nos ponemos
nosotras nos llamamos	nos vamos	nos ponemos
ustedes se llaman	se van	se ponen
ellos se llaman	se van	se ponen
ellas se llaman	se van	se ponen

EJEMPLOS:

Estas señoritas se llaman Luisa y Patricia.
Nosotros nos vamos a las seis.
(Nosotros) Nos vamos a las seis.
Después de la lección, yo me voy a mi casa.
(Yo) Me voy a mi casa.
Para escribir la carta, María se pone delante de la máquina.

EJEMPLOS EN LA FORMA NEGATIVA:

¡Yo no me llamo Cristóbal Colón!
¡(Yo) No me llamo Cristóbal Colón!
Usted no se va a Italia para estudiar el español.
Nosotros no nos ponemos de pie en el coche.
(Nosotros) No nos ponemos de pie en el coche.

Exercise 14

OTROS VERBOS REFLEXIVOS (regulares o irregulares):

LEVANTARse (= ponerse de pie): Después de la lección, los estudiantes se levantan y se van.
DIVERTIRse (tipo E ⟶ IE): Yo me divierto mucho en las fiestas españolas.
SENTARse (tipo E ⟶ IE): María se sienta en la silla.

2. Oral exercise
Conjugate two or three reflexive verbs orally.

ESCENA 15

HACEMOS MUCHOS PROGRESOS

We're Making a Lot of Progress

Juan *Escuche. No repita.*

Pedro – ¡Bueno! Estoy sentado delante de la máquina de escribir, y escribo el nombre del profesor: S - A - N - CH - O.
La letra C y **la letra H** están **juntas,** ¿verdad, María?

María – Sí, la letra C y la letra H están juntas. **Forman la letra CH**.

juntas – together, attached (feminine plural)
forman – they form
CH and **LL** are separate letters of the Spanish alphabet, and have separate sections in the dictionary. So don't look under **C** or **L.**

Pedro	– Sí, y **la letra L** y otra letra L forman **la letra LL: por ejemplo**, en "si*ll*a", "e*ll*a", "ape*ll*ido", etc.
María	– Sí, la letra LL es una letra **doble**. ¡Pero usted siempre escribe **tan** lentamente, Pedro!
Pedro	– Sí, lo sé, lo sé. Ahora, escribo el apellido de mi profesor: García, G - A - R - S …
María	– No, no, no: no es con **una S**, es con **una C**. G - A - R - *C* - Í - A. ¡En Madrid, no es "Garsía", es "García"!
Pedro	– ¡Ah! Sí, en Madrid, "Gar*cí*a". ¡Pero aquí, García!
María	– Sí, claro: García también es correcto.

García – In Spain, this **c** is pronounced with the tip of the tongue between the teeth. However, in Latin America, it is pronounced like **s.**

el alfabeto
The Spanish alphabet is made up of 29 letters. **CH, LL,** and **Ñ** have separate sections in the dictionary.
Ñ is pronounced like the **ni** in **onion.** It's written with a mark called a tilde over it.
The other letters are the same as in English, but several are pronounced quite differently.
B, for example, is pronounced more softly.
C is usually pronounced **k.** But before **e** or **i,** it is pronounced in Spain like the English **th** in **thin,** with the tip of the tongue between the teeth; in Latin America, like **s.**
CH is pronounced **tch,** as in English.
E, never silent, generally sounds like the **e** in **bell.** Ex.: **el alfabeto.**
J has a sound not used in English, like a very strong **h,** well back in the throat.
R is rolled; **U** is pronounced like the **oo** in **moon; V** is pronounced softly, much like the Spanish **B.**
Z, in Spain, is pronounced like **C** before **e** or **i;** in Latin America, like **s.**

Juan — *Repita* **el alfabeto en español:**

A - B - C - CH - D …

E - F - G - H - I …

J - K - L - LL …

M - N - Ñ …

O - P - Q - R …

S - T - U - V - W …

X - Y - Z.

Conteste: ¿Sabe usted el alfabeto? – Sí, yo sé …

Juanita — – Sí, yo sé el alfabeto.

Juan — *Escuche. No repita*. Usted sabe el alfabeto.

¿Y Pedro? Ahora, el profesor pregunta **si** Pedro sabe el alfabeto:

El profesor pregunta si ... – The teacher is asking if ...

Sr. García	– Pedro, ¿sabe usted el alfabeto?
Pedro	– ¿En español?
Sr. García	– ¡Claro, en español! ¿Lo sabe?
Pedro	– Sí, lo sé: A - B - C ...
Sr. García	– Después de la C viene la CH.
Pedro	– ¡Ah! Sí, A - B - C - CH - D - E - F - G - H - I - J - K - L ... ¿Después de la L?
Sr. García	– Después de la L viene la LL.
Pedro	– ¡Ah! Sí, LL. M - N - Ñ - O - P - Q - R - S - T - U - V ...
Sr. García	– W.
Pedro	– ¡Ah, sí! W - X - Y - Z.

Juan — *Conteste*: Pedro sabe el alfabeto, ¿no?

Juanita — – Sí, Pedro sabe el alfabeto.

– Sí, sabe las letras **del** alfabeto.

Del is a contraction of **de** and **el.**

Juan — *Repita*: Él sabe **cuáles** son las letras.

cuáles – which. Plural of the pronoun **cuál.**

Juanita — – Él sabe cuáles son las letras.

Juan — *Escuche.*

¡Estupendo! – Great! Super! Wonderful!
Ya sabe. – You (polite singular) already know.
muchas cosas – many things
hablar – to speak
amable – kind
todavía no – not yet
I don't know how to type yet.
Soy demasiado lento. – I'm too slow (masculine). A girl or woman would say **soy demasiado lenta.** Here **demasiado** is an adverb, so it doesn't change.

Sr. García	– ¡Estupendo! Ud. ya sabe muchas **cosas**, Pedro: sabe cuáles son las letras del alfabeto, sabe **hablar** y escribir en español, sabe **contar** en español: 1, 2, 3, 4, 5, **etc., etc. …**
Pedro	– Gracias, es usted muy **amable**, profesor, pero todavía no sé escribir a máquina. Soy demasiado **lento**.
Sr. García	– Con **el tiempo**, Pedro …
María	– ¡Claro! Con **el tiempo** y con práctica, **poco a poco …**

con el tiempo – in time, with time
poco a poco – little by little

Juan — *Repita*: yo sé, usted sabe, él sabe, ella sabe, ellos saben, **ellas saben, ustedes saben.**

ellas saben – they (feminine) know
ustedes saben – you (polite plural) know

Juan — *Escuche*.

sabemos – we know

Pedro	– Entonces, usted y yo sabemos el alfabeto.
María	– Sí, nosotros sabemos el alfabeto.
Pedro	– Sabemos contar y **sabemos** contestar las preguntas. ¡Pero escribir a máquina, sólo usted, María! ¡Yo no!

sólo usted – only you. We recognize the adverb by its written accent. **Solo** means alone.

Juan — *Repita*: nosotros sabemos contestar.

Y usted también, Sr., Sra. o Srta., usted también sabe contestar.

Sr., Sra. o Srta. = señor, señora o señorita.
These titles are used to address you, the readers.

Lo hace muy bien.

Lo hace muy bien. – You're doing it very well.

Pedro	– ¡Es **verdaderamente** fantástico! **Hacemos muchos progresos**.

verdaderamente – really. This long word is stressed on the next-to-last syllable (**men**), as are all adverbs ending in **-mente.**

•••

FIN DE LA **ESCENA** 15

Exercise 15

1. Irregular verbs ending in **-zco,** 1st-person singular present indicative

DESAPARECER	OBEDECER	RECONOCER
yo desaparezco	**obedezco**	**reconozco**
usted (él, ella) desaparece	obedece	reconoce
nosotros, nosotras desaparecemos	obedecemos	reconocemos
ustedes (ellos, ellas) desaparecen	obedecen	reconocen

PRODUCIR	CONDUCIR	TRADUCIR
yo produzco	**conduzco**	**traduzco**
usted (él, ella) produce	conduce	traduce
nosotros, nosotras producimos	conducimos	traducimos
ustedes (ellos, ellas) producen	conducen	traducen

2. Complete the sentences with the verbs shown.

1. El buen estudiante (OBEDECER) __________________ a su profesor.
2. El actor (APARECER) __________________ en el escenario del teatro.
3. Yo no (RECONOCER) __________________ a este actor. ¿Quién es?
4. Yo (CONDUCIR) __________________ el coche de mi amigo Jorge.
5. Nosotros no (TRADUCIR) __________________ el texto al inglés.
6. Esta máquina (PRODUCIR) __________________ fotocopias.

CORRECCIÓN.

1. El buen estudiante *obedece* a su profesor.
2. El actor *aparece* en el escenario del teatro.
3. Yo *no reconozco* a este actor. ¿Quién es?
4. Yo *conduzco* el coche de mi amigo Jorge.
5. Nosotros *no traducimos* el texto al inglés.
6. Esta máquina *produce* fotocopias.

ESCENA 16

¿QUÉ DIA ES HOY?

What Day Is It Today?

Juan *Escuche. No repita.*

María	– ¡Ay, **madre mía!**¡ ¡**Cuánto trabajo**! ¡Cuánto trabajo tengo!
Pedro	– ¡**Hoy** no es domingo, María!
María	– No, ¡**eso sí que no!** hoy no es domingo, hoy es un día de trabajo.

hoy – today

¡Madre mía! – Good grief! Literally: mother of mine!
¡Cuánto trabajo! – So much work!
tengo – I have
¡Eso sí que no! – No way! I should say not!

un día – one day
semana – week
el lunes – on Monday
lunes – Monday
martes – Tuesday
miércoles – Wednesday
jueves – Thursday
viernes – Friday
sábado – Saturday
domingo – Sunday

Juan — Hoy es **un día de semana.**

Repita: **el lunes** es un día de semana.

El martes es un día de semana.

El miércoles es un día de semana.

Repita: lunes, martes, miércoles, **jueves, viernes,** sábado y domingo.

Conteste: ¿Son éstos los días de la semana?

Juanita — – Sí, éstos son los días de la semana. *Repita*.

– Sí, éstos son los días de la semana.

comienza – begins

Juan — La semana **comienza** el lunes.

hay – there is, there are (invariable form of **haber**)
siete días – seven days

Pedro — – Lunes, martes, miércoles, jueves, viernes, sábado y domingo. 1, 2, 3, 4, 5, 6, 7: en una semana **hay** siete **días.**

Juan — Hay siete días.

Hay siete días en una semana.

Escuche. No repita.

Pedro	– Pero usted, María, no trabaja los siete días de la semana, ¿verdad? No trabaja **ni** el sábado **ni** el domingo.
María	– No trabajo el domingo pero **sí** trabajo el sábado **por la mañana.**
Pedro	– ¿Usted trabaja el sábado?
María	– Sólo por la mañana. Trabajo el sábado por la mañana pero **termino** de trabajar a las doce: después de las doce, no trabajo. No trabajo el sábado **por la tarde.**

ni … ni … – neither … nor …
pero sí trabajo – but I do work (emphatic)
por la mañana – in the morning
el sábado por la mañana – on Saturday morning
termino de … – I finish …
a las doce – at noon
por la tarde – in the afternoon

Juan *Repita*: el sábado por la tarde.

El sábado por **la noche.**

por la noche – in the evening, at night

El sábado por la mañana.

Repita: la mañana, la tarde, la noche.

Conteste: ¿Trabaja María el sábado por la mañana? –

Sí, María trabaja …

Juanita – Sí, María trabaja el sábado por la mañana.

Juan ¿Trabaja ella el sábado por la tarde?

Juanita – No, ella no trabaja el sábado por la tarde.

Juan ¿Va ella a la oficina el domingo?

– No, ella no va …

Juanita – No, ella no va a la oficina el domingo.

Juan Pero hoy no es domingo (¡escuche!): hoy todo el

todo el mundo – everyone (the whole world)

mundo trabaja en la oficina.

el número de teléfono – the telephone number. Notice the two written accents.

Sr. López	– ¡María!
María	– Sí, Sr. López.
Sr. López	– No tengo **el número de teléfono** del Sr. Johnson. ¿**Lo** tiene usted?
María	– Sí. Es 44-58-31.
Sr. López	– 44-58-31. Gracias.

¿Cuál es su número? – What's your (phone) number?

Juan *Conteste*: 44-58-31, ¿es su número, el número de usted?

Juanita – No, no es mi número.

Juan ¿Es el número del Sr. Johnson?

Juanita – Sí, es el número del Sr. Johnson.

Juan ¿Cuál es **su número de usted**?

Juanita – Mi número es: ....

Juan ¡Ah! Muy bien.

Escuche. No repita.

María	– El número de teléfono del Sr. Johnson es éste, pero ahora él no está aquí.
Sr. López	– ¿Dónde está?

María	– En **Colombia.**
Sr. López	– ¿Está en Colombia?
María	– Sí. Está en la ciudad de **Bogotá.**
Sr. López	– ¿**Tenemos** su **dirección** en Bogotá?
María	– Sí. La dirección del Sr. Johnson está en la computadora. ¡Ah! ¡Aquí tengo la dirección! "Sr. William Johnson Avenida de la Independencia, 32 Bogotá, Colombia."

Colombia – Colombia

Bogotá – Notice the written accent.

la dirección – the address
tenemos – we have

Juan *Conteste*: ¿Sabe María la dirección del Sr. Johnson?

Juanita – Sí, María sabe la dirección del Sr. Johnson.

Juan ¿En qué país está el Sr. Johnson?

¿En Colombia o en Chile?

Chile – Chile. As in English, **ch** is pronounced **tch; e** has the sound of the **e** in **pep.**

Juanita – El Sr. Johnson está en Colombia.

Juan ¿En qué ciudad está?

Juanita – Está en Bogotá.

Ahora *escuche.*

Pedro	– María, ¿qué hora es? Hoy **no tengo reloj,** y el reloj de la oficina **se ha parado.**
María	– Son las doce.
Pedro	– ¿**Ya** son las doce? Entonces ya es **hora de parar**, ¿no?
Sr. López	– Sí, es verdad, Pedro. María, pare de trabajar. Pare una hora.

Hoy no tengo reloj. – I don't have my watch (on) today.
Se ha parado. – It's stopped.
ya – already
hora de parar – quitting time (at work)
Pare. – Stop (for an hour). Imperative polite **you.**

María	– Muy bien, pero sólo una hora porque hoy tengo mucho trabajo.

Hemos trabajado mucho. – We've done a lot of work. (We've worked a lot.)

¡Hasta luego! See you later!

Juan — *Escuche*. Nosotros también **hemos trabajado** mucho. Es hora de **parar** esta cassette. ¡Hasta luego!

•••

FIN DE LA **ESCENA 16**

Exercise 16

1. *Tú* and the 2nd-person singular of some other regular verbs

COMPRENDER	usted comprende	= (familiar) *tú* comprendes
APRENDER	usted aprende	= (fam.) tú aprendes
PROMETER	usted promete	= tú prometes
VENDER	usted vende	= tú vendes
ABRIR	usted abre	= tú abres
ASISTIR	usted asiste	= tú asistes
DECIDIR	usted decide	= tú decides
DESCRIBIR	usted describe	= tú describes
ESCRIBIR	usted escribe	= tú escribes
DIVIDIR	usted divide	= tú divides
OMITIR	usted omite	= tú omites

IRse (*verbo reflexivo*) usted se va = tú *te* vas

2. Direct object pronoun

ME, TE, LO, LA, NOS, LOS, LAS.

Yo tomo *el libro*	= Yo *lo* tomo.	("lo" remplaza "el libro")
Yo tomo *la carta*	= Yo *la* tomo.	("la" remplaza "la carta")
Yo tomo *los libros*	= Yo *los* tomo.	("los" remplaza "los libros")
Yo tomo *las cartas*	= Yo *las* tomo.	("las" remplaza "las cartas")

Otros ejemplos: Usted *me* mira.
Pedro *nos* mira.
Yo *te* miro.

Exercise 16

Ejemplos en la forma negativa

Yo *no te miro.*

Tú no *me* miras.

Yo no *lo* miro.

Yo no *la* miro.

Usted no *nos* escucha.

Yo no *los* escucho.

Nosotros no *las* escuchamos.

Ejemplos en el Pretérito perfecto

Yo *te he mirado.*

Tú *me* has mirado.

Yo *lo* he mirado.

Yo *la* he mirado.

Usted *nos* ha escuchado.

Yo *los* he escuchado.

Nosotros *las* hemos escuchado.

Nosotros *no las hemos escuchado* (Pretérito perfecto y negativo.)

ESCENA 17

LA SALIDA A LA CALLE — Going Out

María	– ... Y hay muchísimos coches en las calles y **policías** por todas partes.
Alberto	– ¿Viene usted **de** la oficina?
María	– No, vengo **de** mi casa.
Alberto	– Y ahora, ¿qué hora es?
María	– Las ocho y media.
Alberto	– ¡Bueno¡ Ya es hora de **cerrar** la tienda. Señoras y señores, **cerramos.** ¡Cerramos!

muchísimos coches – lots and lots of cars. **Muchísimo** is the superlative form of the adjective **mucho / a** – many.
policías – police officers
vengo de – I'm coming from. From the verb **venir.**
cerrar – to close
cierra – he's closing
Present tense of the verb **cerrar: cierro, cierras, cierra, cerramos, cerráis, cierran**

Juan	Alberto **cierra** la tienda.
	Conteste: ¿Cierra la puerta?
Juanita	– Sí, cierra la puerta.
Juan	¿La puerta de la casa o la puerta de la tienda?
Juanita	– La puerta de la tienda.
Juan	*Repita*: ahora, la tienda está **cerrada.**
	No está **abierta.** Está cerrada.

cerrada – closed (feminine)

No está abierta. – It isn't open (feminine).

Una señora	– Por favor, señor, quisiera comprar un disco. ¿Está abierta la tienda?
Alberto	– No, señora. La tienda está cerrada. Es demasiado **tarde.**
La señora	– ¡Oh!
Alberto	– Venga **mañana.**
La señora	– ¿A qué hora **abren por la mañana**?
Alberto	– **Abrimos** a las nueve.

quisiera comprar – I'd like to buy Here we find **quisiera,** the past subjunctive of **querer,** followed by a verb in the infinitive. This construction is essential for polite requests. Ex.: **Por favor, quisiera saber si ...** – Please, I'd like to know if ...
demasiado – too (excessively)
venga – come. Imperative of the verb **venir** – to come; 3rd-person singular, for the polite **you.**
¿A qué hora abren por la mañana? – What time do you open in the morning?
abrimos – we open. **Abren** and **abrimos** are two forms of the verb **abrir.**

Juan *Escuche. No repita.*

Alberto **ha cerrado** la tienda,

y ahora va con María **por** la

avenida. Alberto y María **van** juntos.

por la avenida – along the avenue. **Por** is used after a verb to indicate movement within a given space.

María	– ¿Adónde **vamos**?
Alberto	– **Vamos al cine.**

Juan *Repita*: **el cine** está en la avenida.

Conteste: ¿Van ellos a la oficina?

Juanita – No, ellos no van a la oficina.

Juan ¿Van a la escuela?

Juanita – No, no van a la escuela.

Juan ¿Van a **la biblioteca** o al cine?

Juanita – Van al cine.

Juan *Repita*: ellos van – ustedes van …

Yo voy – Nosotros vamos …

Él va – Usted va …

Van al cine. – They're going to the movies. From the verb **ir** – to go.

Alberto	– **Vamos a ver** una película en el cine de la avenida.

vamos a ver – we're going to see. This expression is used frequently, with or without a word or words following the verb.

Juan *Conteste*: ¿**Van a comprar** discos?

Juanita – No, no van a comprar discos.

Juan ¿**Van a escuchar** la radio?

Juanita – No, no van a escuchar la radio.

Juan ¿**Van a mirar** la televisión?

Juanita – No, no van a mirar la televisión.

María – ¿Qué película vamos a ver?
Alberto – Esta: **"Aventura en Nueva York."**
María – ¡Ah, sí! **Dicen** que es muy **buena**.
Alberto – Vamos a **sacar las entradas ...**

dicen – they say
The indefinite **they** is expressed in Spanish:
by the 3rd-person plural: **dicen** – they say
by **se** and the 3rd-person singular: **se dice** – they say
sacar las entradas – get the tickets

Juan *Escuche. No repita.*

Alberto y María **van a ver**

"Aventura en Nueva York",

una película americana en el cine de la avenida.

¡**Buenas noches,** Alberto!

¡Buenas noches, María!

¡**Diviértanse**!

Juanita ... ¡Y buenas noches también a todos

los que escuchan esta cassette!

Si van al cine o **si hacen otra salida**

Buenas noches. – Good evening.
¡Diviértanse! – Have a good time!
This imperative is used to speak to two or more people. The **e** in the root of **divertirse** changes to **ie** in several forms of the verb.
Me divierto. – I'm having a good time.
Diviértanse is the 3rd-person plural imperative. The reflexive pronoun **se** is added to the end of the verb, as in **sentarse** – to sit down.
todos los que – all (those) who
si – if. Conjunction of condition.
si van – if you (polite plural) are going
si hacen – if you're making (another trip). 3rd-person plural, for the polite **you.**

¡diviértanse!

Juan ¡A todos, **muy buenas noches**!

•••

FIN DE LA **ESCENA 17**

Exercise 17

1. Present and present perfect tenses of the verbs:

VER		**IR**	
Presente	*Préterito perfecto*	*Presente*	*Préterito perfecto*
Yo veo	Yo he visto	Yo voy	he ido
Tú ves	Tú has visto	Tú vas	has ido
Usted ve	Usted ha visto	Usted va	ha ido
Él ve	Él ha visto	Él va	ha ido
Ella ve	Ella ha visto	Ella va	ha ido
Nosotros vemos	Nosotros hemos visto	Nosostros vamos	hemos ido
Ustedes ven	Ustedes han visto	Ustedes van	han ido
Ellos ven	Ellos han visto	Ellos van	han ido
Ellas ven	Ellas han visto	Ellas van	han ido

Future (immediate):
Verb *ir* + preposition *a* + verb in the infinitive
Ex: *Voy a estudiar*: I'm going to study

Yo voy a escuchar la escena número **22**.
Yo voy a contestar las preguntas.
Voy a repetir el vocabulario.
Voy a ver una película en la televisión.
Tú vas a cantar una canción en español.
Usted va a salir con su amiga esta noche.
El turista va a visitar la catedral de Burgos.
Nosotros vamos a vender nuestro coche.
Ellos van a telefonear.
Ustedes no van a contestar en inglés.

ESCENA 18

UNA INVITACIÓN — An Invitation

Juan — *No repita.* Hoy es viernes. Son las seis de la tarde. En esta oficina, todo el mundo para **de trabajar** a las seis. **Todos los empleados terminan** a las seis de la tarde. Como ya son las seis y diez, todos **han terminado** y ahora, todos **salen** de la oficina.

para de trabajar – stops working (gets off work)
todos los empleados – all the employees
como ya son ... – since it's already ... (ten after six). The conjunction **como** has no written accent.
salen – they're leaving. From the verb **salir** – to leave (to go out of). You'll often see this sign: **Salida** – Exit.

cenar – to eat (the evening meal), to dine
con mucho gusto – with great pleasure

conozco – I know. Verb **conocer,** with a change in the root consonant.
de cuando en cuando – from time to time
la dirección – the address. Be careful with this word.
también viene – you are coming too (polite singular)
con mi señora – with my wife
¡Estupendo! – Great! Wonderful!
padre – father
madre – mother. Children say **papá y mamá.**
Hasta luego. – See you soon.

Sr. López	– ¿María, viene usted a mi casa para **cenar** esta noche?
María	– Sí, señor, **con mucho gusto.** Vengo con mi amigo Alberto. **Usted conoce** a Alberto, ¿no?
Sr. López	– Sí, **conozco** a Alberto. Él viene a la oficina **de cuando en cuando...** ¿Tiene usted la dirección de mi casa?
María	– Sí, señor.
Sr. López	– Y usted, Sr. García, también viene, ¿verdad?
Sr. García	– Sí, a las ocho y media, con **mi señora**.
Sr. López	– ¿Tienen ustedes mi dirección?
Sr. García	– Sí.
Sr. López	– ¡**Estupendo**!
María	– ¿Y Pedro? ¿Viene también?
Sr. López	– Sí. Viene con su **padre** y con su **madre**. Bueno, ¡hasta luego!
María	– Hasta luego, Sr. López.

sus padres – their parents
a casa del Sr. López – at Mr. López's house

Juan — Esta noche, el Sr. y la Sra. García, María y su amigo Alberto, Pedro y **sus padres van a cenar a casa del Sr. López**.

Conteste: ¿**Van** ellos al restaurante?

Juanita — – No, no van al restaurante.

Juan — *Repita*: todos van a cenar **a casa** del Sr. López.

Escuche. Ahora estamos en la casa del Sr. y la Sra. López. Ella está en **la cocina** y **prepara la cena** para esta noche.

la cocina – the kitchen
Prepara la cena. – She's preparing dinner.

Repita: La Sra. López está en la cocina.

La Sra. López prepara la cena.

La cena es **la comida** de la noche.

la comida – the meal

La comida del **mediodía** se llama **el almuerzo** y la primera comida del día es **el desayuno**.

del mediodía – at noon
el almuerzo – lunch
el desayuno – breakfast

Conteste: ¿Cuántas comidas hay en un día, una, dos o tres? – En un día, hay ...

¿cuántas comidas? – how many meals?

Juanita – En un día, hay tres comidas.

Juan *Conteste*: ¿Quién prepara la cena, el Sr. López o su señora?

Juanita – Su señora prepara la cena.

Juan ¿Cómo se llama **la esposa** del director, Sra. García o Sra. López?

la esposa – his wife. In some places **la mujer** is used, often informally.

Juanita – La esposa del director se llama Sra. López.

Sra. López	– Preparar una cena **tan** grande es mucho trabajo.

tan grande – so big
mucho trabajo – a lot of work. **Mucho** is an adjective, so it agrees in gender and number with the noun it modifies: **mucho, mucha, muchos, muchas.**

Juan *Conteste*: ¿Tiene mucho trabajo la Sra. López?

Juanita – Sí, tiene mucho trabajo.

Juan	¿Tiene mucho trabajo en la cocina?
Juanita	– Sí, tiene mucho trabajo en la cocina.

llaman – someone's ringing the bell. Literally: They're calling. Impersonal 3rd-person plural.
en seguida – right away

Sra. López	– ¡Ah, **llaman a la puerta**! ¡Un momento, por favor! ¡Voy en seguida!

Juan	*Conteste*: ¿A dónde va la Sra. López, a la puerta o a la ventana?
Juanita	– Va a la puerta.

ven – come. Familiar 2nd-person singular imperative of the verb **venir.** We've already encountered the 3rd-person singular imperative **venga,** for the polite **you.**
ese perro – that dog

Sra. López	– ¡Sandy! ¡Sandy, **ven** aquí! ¡Ay!...¡Ese perro!

Juan	*Conteste*: ¿Como se llama el perro del Sr. y la Sra. López?
Juanita	– El perro del Sr. y la Sra. López se llama "Sandy".
Juan	¿Está el perro en la casa o en la oficina?
Juanita	– El perro está en la casa.
Juan	*Repita*: el perro se queda en la casa.

Sra. López – ¡Sandy, **quédate** aquí! ¡**Quédate** aquí!...

¡Quédate aquí! – Stay here! Familiar 2nd-person imperative of the reflexive verb **quedarse** – to stay, to remain.
quedarse – to stay:
me quedo – I'm staying; **te quedas** – you're staying (familiar); **se queda** – he or she is staying, you (polite) are staying

•••

FIN DE LA **ESCENA 18**

Exercise 18

1. Demonstrative adjectives

	Singular	Plural	
	ESTE....., ESTA.....,	ESTOS.....,	ESTAS......,
(o:	ESE......, ESA.....,	ESOS......,	ESAS.......)

Este muchacho se llama Alberto y *ese muchacho* se llama Felipe.
Esta muchacha se llama Dolores y *esa muchacha* se llama Cristina.
Estos muchachos son mejicanos y *esos muchachos* son argentinos.
Estas muchachas son colombianas y *esas muchachas* son venezolanas.

2. Demonstrative pronouns

	ÉSTE, ÉSTA,	ÉSTOS, ÉSTAS,
(o:	ÉSE, ÉSA,	ÉSOS, ÉSAS.)

Éste se llama Alberto, y *ése* se llama Felipe.
Ésta se llama Dolores, y *ésa* se llama Cristina.
Éstos son mejicanos, y *ésos* son argentinos.
Éstas son colombianas, y *ésas* son venezolanas.

3. Complete the sentences with demonstrative adjectives or pronouns.

1. __________ reloj es de Pedro, y __________ es de María.
2. __________ silla es de Pedro, y __________ es de María.
3. __________ papeles son del Sr. García, y __________ son del Sr. López.
4. __________ máquinas son buenas, pero __________ son malas.
5. Hoy es sábado: María no trabaja __________ tarde.
6. Yo tengo cita con mis amigos __________ domingo.
7. __________ escena es la escena número 23, y __________ es la 24.
8. __________ pregunta es fácil, pero __________ es difícil.
9. ¡ __________ ejercicios no son difíciles, son fáciles!
10. __________ ejercicio ha terminado, y __________ otro empieza.

Exercise 18

CORRECCION.

1. Este *reloj* es de Pedro, y ése es de María.
2. Esta *silla* ... y ésa
3. Estos *papeles* ... y ésos
4. Estas *máquinas* ... pero ésas
5. esta tarde
6. este domingo
7. Esta *escena* ... y ésa
8. Esta *pregunta* ... pero ésa
9. Estos *ejercicios*
10. Este *ejercicio* y ése otro ...

ESCENA 19

¡BIENVENIDOS! Welcome!

Juan	El Sr. y la Sra. García **llegan** a la casa de la Sra. López. Llegan con el Sr. López.	**llegan** – they're here (arriving) The verb **llegar** (to arrive) begins with **ll,** which has its own section in the dictionary.
	Llaman a la puerta.	
	La Sra. López abre la puerta y dice:	
Sra. López	– ¡Buenas noches, Sra. García! ¡Buenas noches, Sr. García! **¡Bienvenidos!** ¡Hola, Carlos!	**¡Bienvenidos!** – Welcome! **Hola.** – Hi. Hello.

el nombre – the first (given) name

Juan — "Carlos" es el nombre del Sr. López.

Sra. López – ¡**Entren**! ¡Entren, por favor!

Han llegado. – They've arrived. The past participle (**llegado**) doesn't change.
Entran. – They're coming in.

Juan — El Sr. García y la Sra. García **han llegado** a la casa.

Ahora **entran** con el Sr. López.

Sra. López – ¡Hola, Carlos!

Entra en su casa. – He's going into his house.
la entrada – the entrance
Entrada / Salida – Entrance / Exit

Juan — *Conteste*: El Sr. Carlos López entra en su casa, ¿verdad? – Sí, …

Juanita — – Sí, el Sr. Carlos López entra en su casa.

Juan — ¿Entra solo o con amigos?

Juanita — – Entra con amigos.

Vengan – Come. Verb **venir,** 3rd-person plural, the polite **you** (**ustedes**).
Siéntense. – Sit down. Mrs. López uses **vengan** and **sienten** to speak to more than one person (Mr. and Mrs. García).
aquí tienen – here you have … (**ustedes tienen**)
sillas – chairs
un sofá – a sofa

Sra. López – ¿Cómo está usted, Sr. García?
Sr. García – Bien, gracias. ¿Y usted?
Sra. López – Muy bien. **Vengan** por aquí y **siéntense:** aquí tienen sillas y **un sofá** muy cómodo.

	¡Por favor, **siéntense**!
Sra. García	– ¡Sra. López, su casa es muy bonita!
Sra. López	– Gracias. No es muy grande pero es cómoda.

Juan *Repita*: ¡Por favor, siéntense!

Sr. López	– Hay sillas pero el sofá es **más** cómodo. ¡Por favor, siéntense en el sofá!

más cómodo – more comfortable

Juan *Repita*: Es más cómodo.

Es más grande y más cómodo.

Sra. López	– ¿**Un cóctel**? ¿**Un aperitivo**?
Sr. García	– Sí, **con mucho gusto**.
Sra. López	– ¿Y usted, Sra. García? ¿**Toma usted algo**? ¿Un cóctel? ¿Un aperitivo?
Sra. García	– No, para mí, **nada**, gracias.
Sr. López	– ¿No toma usted nada?
Sra. García	– No, **antes de comer**, yo **no** tomo **nada**.
Sra. García	– Nada. Nada **en absoluto**.
Sr. Lopez	– ¿**De verdad**?
Sra. García	– Sí, de verdad.
Sra. López	– ¡Carlos, el teléfono! ¡Contest**a** el teléfono! ¡Yo estoy ocupada en la cocina! ...

un cóctel – a cocktail. Notice the Spanish spelling.
un aperitivo – an aperitif
¿Toma usted algo? – Would you like something to drink? Like **nada,** its opposite, **algo** is an invariable indefinite pronoun.
nada – nothing. It's used without any other negative when it goes before a verb; when it follows a verb, it requires **no.**
nada – nothing; **no ... nada** – not ... anything. Literally: not nothing.
antes de comer – before eating
No tomo nada. – I'm not drinking anything.

Sr. López – Sí, sí, ya voy … **Con permiso.**

Sr. y Sra. García – Sí, claro. **¡Cómo no!**

Sr. López – ¿Diga? ¿Cómo? … ¡**No entiendo**! … ¿Quién habla? … **No entiendo nada**. ¿Quién? … ¡Ah, … es usted, Pedro! … ¿Que no tiene mi dirección? … **Pues** escuche, Pedro: no hay **problema**; ¿Tiene usted su bolígrafo? ¿Sí? Entonces **tome** un papel y **escriba** mi dirección. Es: **calle Bolívar**, 16. ¿Viene usted en seguida? … ¿Con su padre y con su madre? … ¡**Estupendo**! Hasta **pronto**.

No entiendo nada. – I don't understand anything.

pues – well, then
No hay problema. – There's no problem.
bolígrafo – (ballpoint) pen
entonces – then
Tome un papel. – Take a sheet of paper. 3rd-person singular imperative of **tomar** – to take; for the polite **you.**
calle Bolívar 16 – 16 Bolívar Street. The number goes after the name of the street.
hasta – until, up to
Hasta pronto. – See you soon.

Juan *Repita*: Pedro **ha llamado** por teléfono.

Juanita – Pedro ha llamado por teléfono.

– Pedro ha **telefoneado**.

ha telefoneado – he's telephoned

Juan ¿Y quién ha **contestado**?

ha contestado – he's answered
he contestado – I've answered

Juanita – Ha contestado el Sr. López.

Juan *Escuche* el verbo en **el presente** y en **el pasado** y repita: Pedro llama … Pedro ha llamado.

Pedro escucha … Pedro ha **escuchado**.

he escuchado – I've listened

El Sr. López contesta … El Sr. López ha contestado.

Juanita – ¡Yo también contesto las preguntas! …

Yo contesto … Yo **he** contestado.

Hablo español … He **hablado** español.

Juan — Pedro y el Sr. López **han** hablado.

Han hablado, han escuchado, han contestado.

Pedro, su padre y su madre han **llegado**.

Han llegado a la casa del Sr. López.

Sr. López	– ¡Buenas noches! ¡Entren!
Pedro	– Sr. López, **le presento** a mi padre y a mi madre.
Sr. López	– ¡**Encantado**!
La madre de Pedro.	– ¡**Encantada**!
El padre de Pedro.	– ¡**Mucho gusto**, Sr. López!

le presento – let me introduce
le – 3rd-person singular pronoun, used to express an object in both masculine and feminine forms.
Le is used here for the polite **you.**
Encantado, encantada. – I'm pleased (masculine and feminine) to meet you.

•••

FIN DE LA **ESCENA 19**

Exercise 19

1. Comparatives

1 Comparative of superiority MÁS + adjetivo (o adverbio) + QUE

Ejemplos: El sofá es *más* cómodo q*ue* la silla.
La gramática es *más* difícil q*ue* el vocabulario.
María escribe *más* rápidamente q*ue* Pedro.

---

2 Comparative of inferiority MENOS + adjetivo + QUE

Ejemplos: Los ejercicios son *menos* interesantes *que* las escenas.
La gramática es *menos* divertida *que* el vocabulario.

---

3 Comparative of equality TAN + adjetivo + COMO

Ejemplos: ¡Pero la gramática es *tan* importante *como* el vocabulario!
El ejercicio 24 no es *tan* divertido *como* la escena 24.
La escena 23 no es *tan* larga *como* la escena 24.
(o: La escena 23 es más corta que la escena 24).

2. Indefinite pronouns *algo* and *nada*: something and nothing

- Yo escribo *algo* en español (¡Escribo las frases de los ejercicios!).
- Yo *no* escribo *nada* en inglés (¡Aquí, sólo escribo en español!).

- ¿Hay *algo* en la mesa? ¿Un libro? ¿Un papel? ¿Un bolígrafo? … ¿ALGO?
- No. *No* hay *nada* en la mesa. No hay absolutamente NADA.

- La señora García come mucho, pero no bebe vino, no bebe sangría, no bebe champán: ella *no* bebe *nada*.
- Yo miro por la ventana, pero no veo coches, no veo bicicletas: yo *no* veo *nada*.
- Yo escucho la cassette, pero *no* oigo *nada* durante la "pausa de cinco segundos": no oigo música, no oigo teléfonos, no oigo máquinas de escribir … *No* se oye *nada* entre dos escenas. ¡Nada … más que el metrónomo! (¡Siempre el mismo metrónomo!)

ESCENA 20

FLORES PARA LA SEÑORA DE LA CASA

Sra. López	– ¡Ah! Llaman a la puerta. ¡Sandy, **quieto**! Son Alberto y María. ¡**Por fin**!
Alberto	– Estas **flores** son para usted, Sra. López.
Sra. López	– ¡Oh, muchas gracias! Las flores **me gustan** mucho. ¡Y éstas son **rosas**! Las rosas son mis flores **favoritas.** **¡Gracias, Alberto, gracias, María, por la atención**!
Alberto	– Esto no es nada, Sra. López.
Sra. López	– Para mí, es mucho: es una atención muy **delicada**. Gracias.

Flowers for the Lady of the House

¡Quieto!– (Be) still! Mrs. López is telling her dog Sandy to be still.
¡Por fin! – At last!
me gustan – I like. **Las flores me gustan.** – I like flowers.
Éstas son rosas. – These are roses. Remember that **s** is never pronounced like the English **z.**
mis flores favoritas – my favorite flowers. Plural of **mi flor favorita**.
Esto no es nada. – It's nothing. Remember this polite expression. You'll use it when someone thanks you for a service, a favor, or a gift.
Gracias por la atención. – Thanks for (your) kindness (attention). Another

expression that will pleasantly surprise the people you talk to.
para mí – for me. In this case, **para** expresses a point of view.
dar – to give
da – he or she gives
dan – they give

Juan — *Repita*: **una flor**, muchas flores.

Alberto **da** flores a la Sra. López.

Alberto y María **dan** flores a la Sra. López.

Conteste: ¿Qué flores dan a la Sra. López, **margaritas** o rosas?

Juanita — – Dan rosas a la Sra. López.

Ellos le dan rosas. – They're giving her (Mrs. López) roses.
le – 3rd-person indirect object pronoun

Juan — Ellos dan rosas **a la Sra. López**.

Repita: Ellos **le** dan rosas.

Ya estamos todos aquí. – We're all here now.
¡A cenar! – Come to the table! Literally: to dine.
venga – come (singular polite **you**)
en seguida – right away

Sr. López	– Bueno. Ya **estamos** todos aquí.
Sra. López	– Entonces, ¡**a cenar**!
María	– Alberto, **venga**.
Alberto	– En seguida.
Sra. López	– Pedro, venga. ¡**Vamos a cenar**!

Juan — *Repita*: Vamos a cenar.

dice – she says. Verb **decir** — to say.

La Sra. López **dice**: "¡Vamos a cenar!"

Siéntese aquí. – Sit here (**usted**).
Siéntense. – Sit down (**ustedes**).
a la derecha – on the right
a la izquierda – on the left

Sra. López	– Usted, Sra. García, siéntese aquí, por favor. Usted, Sr. García, siéntese aquí, **a la derecha**. Pedro, aquí, **a la izquierda**. Alberto y María, siéntense aquí. Los padres de

> Pedro, aquí. Carlos, **tú**, aquí, delante de mí;
> y yo, aquí.

Juan	*Conteste*: Ahora, ¿cómo están todos, **sentados** o de pie?
Juanita	– Están sentados.
Juan	La mesa es muy grande, ¿verdad?
Juanita	– Sí, la mesa es muy grande.
Juan	*Repita*: El Sr. García está sentado a la derecha. Pedro está a la izquierda.
Juan	¿Y usted? ¿Ahora está usted sentado o de pie? *Conteste*: – Ahora yo estoy …
Juanita	– Ahora yo estoy sentada.
Juan	Yo estoy sentado.

Están sentados. – They (masculine) are seated; **están sentadas** – they (feminine) are seated.
la mesa – the table

o de pie – or standing up

Estoy sentado. – I (masculine) am seated; **estoy sentada** – I (feminine) am seated.
The past participle agrees in number and gender when it's used with any verb but **haber.** Ex.: **Nos quedamos sentadas** – We (feminine plural) remain seated.

Sr. López	– ¿Un poco de **vino**, Sr. García?
Sr. García	– Sí, **con mucho gusto**. Gracias.

un poco de vino – a little wine
con mucho gusto – with great pleasure. This polite expression will be well received when you accept an offer or invitation.

Juan	*Repita*: El Sr. García **bebe** vino.

bebe – he's drinking. Present tense of the verb **beber:**
bebo – I drink; **bebes** – you (**tú**) drink; **bebe** – he or she drinks, you (**usted**) drink; **bebemos** – we drink; **bebéis** – you drink (familiar plural, in Spain); **beben** – they drink or you (**ustedes**) drink

Conteste: ¿Bebe vino o bebe **Coca-Cola**?

Juanita – Bebe vino.

vino tinto – red wine

Sr. López – ¿Vino **blanco** o vino **tinto**?
Sr. García – Tinto, por favor.¡Mmm, … este vino es **buenísimo**!
Sra. García – ¡Y la comida también es **buenísima**, Sra. López! **La paella** es buenísima.
Sra. López – Gracias.

buenísimo – very good, extremely good
The suffix **-ísimo / a** (**os / as** in the plural) is used to form the superlative adjective, which agrees in gender and number with the noun it modifies.
La paella es buenísima. – The paella (a Spanish dish) is excellent.

come – he or she eats. Present tense of the verb **comer: como, comes, come, comemos, coméis, comen**
cerveza – beer
bisté – beefsteak. Notice the spelling.

Juan *Repita*: todo el mundo bebe y **come**.

¿Qué **beben** los invitados, vino o **cerveza**?

Juanita – Beben vino.

Juan ¿Qué **comen**, paella o **bisté**?

Juanita – Comen paella.

Juan *Conteste*: la paella es **una comida típica**, ¿no?

Juanita – Sí, la paella es una comida típica.

un plato típico – a typical dish

Juan *Repita*: la paella es **un plato típico**.

Conteste: ¿Dónde comen **estas personas**, en un restaurante o **en casa de amigos**?

Juanita – Comen en casa de amigos.

en casa de amigos – in the home of some friends. Note: **en casa de** when there's no change of place; **a casa de** when there is a movement toward the place.

Sra. García	– Esta paella **me gusta** mucho.
Sr. García	– Y **a mí me gusta** mucho este vino.
Sr. López	– Es un vino de Rioja.

a mí me gusta mucho – I (emphatic) really like

Juan *Repita*: la paella me gusta.

También me gusta **la ensalada**.

Y **las frutas** también me gustan.

Escuche. No repita.

la ensalada – the salad

María	– ¡**Escuchen**! ¿**Saben ustedes** qué día es hoy? ¿Lo saben?
Todos juntos	– ¿Qué día es?
María	– ¡Hoy es **el 4 de abril**!
Todos juntos	– ¿ Y **qué hay de particular** el 4 de abril?
María	– El 4 de abril es **el aniversario de matrimonio** del Sr. y la Sra. López.
Todos juntos	– ¿De verdad?
Sra. López	– Sí.
Sr. López	– Es nuestro **décimo** aniversario de matrimonio.
Alberto	– ¡Diez años de matrimonio!
Todos juntos (**menos** el Sr. y la Sra. López)	– ¡Feliz aniversario!
Alberto	– **Bebo** a su **salud**.
Sr. García	– **¡Salud!**

¿saben ustedes? – do you know? (plural polite **you**)
Present tense of the verb **saber: sé, sabes, sabe; sabemos, sabéis, saben**
Hoy es el 4 de abril. – Today is the 4th of April.
matrimonio – wedding

décimo / a – tenth (masculine, feminine)

¡Feliz aniversario! – Happy anniversary!

¡Salud! – To your health! Cheers!
esperen – wait. Imperative of **esperar** – to wait; 3rd-person plural, for the polite **you.**
para celebrar – to celebrate
para saber – to know, to find out
When the infinitive is used to express purpose, it's preceded by **para.**

champán – champagne. This word has been "acclimatized" and begins with the **tch** sound.

María	– ¡Salud!
Sr. López	– ¡**Un momento**! **Esperen** un momento: para **celebrar esta ocasión**, voy a **abrir una botella de champán**.

•••

FIN DE LA **ESCENA 20**

Exercise 20

1. Mealtime vocabulary

El desayuno: café con leche (o té) y pan con mantequilla.
El almuerzo: pescado, carne, legumbres, ensalada, queso, postre, vino, café
(y para *la cena* también + la sopa.)

2. Verbs in the present indicative

Yo *escucho* la radio, y ahora *oigo* música moderna.
Yo *miro* la televisión, y ahora *veo* una película argentina.

ESCUCHAR	OÍR	MIRAR	VER
yo escucho	oigo	miro	veo
tú escuchas	oyes	miras	ves
él escucha	oye	mira	ve
nosotros escuchamos	oímos	miramos	vemos
vosotros escucháis	oís	miráis	véis
ellos escuchan	oyen	miran	ven

3. The same verbs in the present perfect tense

he escuchado	he oído	he mirado	he visto
has escuchado	has oído	has mirado	has visto
ha escuchado	ha oído	ha mirado	ha visto
hemos escuchado	hemos oído	hemos mirado	hemos visto
habéis escuchado	habéis oído	habéis mirado	habéis visto
han escuchado	han oído	han mirado	han visto

"*Escuchado*", "*mirado*", "*cantado*", "*bailado*", etc. (para los verbos en "AR") son PARTICIPIOS PASADOS. Otros participios pasados: "*traído*", "*comprendido*", "*entendido*" (para los verbos en "ER") y "*repetido*", "*oído*", "*leído*" (para los verbos en "IR".)

Exercise 20

Note: Here are some irregular past participles:

ABRIR: He *abierto* la puerta.
ESCRIBIR: Tú has *escrito* muchas cartas.
DECIR: Él ha *dicho* la verdad.
HACER: Nosotros hemos *hecho* un error.
PONER: ¡Ustedes no han *puesto* el teléfono en la silla sino en la mesa!

ESCENA 21

EL REGALO

The Gift

Sra. López	– ¡Qué **bonita** es mi caja de música! ¡**Qué bonita**! Gracias, Carlos. Gracias por este regalo **tan bonito.**

Juan *Conteste*: ¿Es bonito el regalo?

Juanita – Sí, es bonito.

Juan Es una caja muy bonita, ¿verdad?

¡Qué bonita es mi caja de música! – How pretty my music box is!
This exclamation includes a verb, so the adjective goes immediately after the exclamatory **qué** (with a written accent).
¡Qué bonita! – How pretty! Here the verb is understood.

regalo – gift. From the verb **regalar** – to give (as a gift).

Juanita – Sí, es una caja muy bonita.

Juan *Repita*: bonito – bonita.

Sr. López – Esta **cajita** de música,
¿**saben ustedes de dónde** viene?
Viene de la tienda de Alberto.
Él vende muchos discos pero también vende cajas de música, como ésta.

como ésta – like this (one). The written accent falls on the **e** in the demonstrative pronoun **ésta,** but on the **a** in **está,** a form of the verb **estar.**

Juan *Escuche. No repita.*

Hoy, día 4 de abril, es **el presente.**

Ayer, día 3 de abril, es **el pasado.**

El presente y el pasado. Hoy y ayer.

Ayer, Alberto **vendió** la caja de música al Sr. López.

Ayer, el Sr. López **compró** la caja.

Repita: Alberto ha vendido o: Alberto vendió.

El Sr. López ha comprado o:

El Sr. López compró.

Repita el pasado de los verbos: él vendió, él compró.

Repita el presente de los verbos: él compra, él vende.

el presente – the present (now)
ayer – yesterday
el pasado – the past

hoy – today

vendió – he or she sold. Preterite (simple past tense) of **vender** – to sell.
compró – he or she bought
In Spanish, as in English, the preterite (simple past) is used to express an action that took place at a given moment in the past. Ex.: **Ayer Alberto vendió la caja.** – Yesterday Albert sold the box. Here **vendió** is preferable to **ha vendido,** although this present perfect tense is more easily conjugated.

María	– El Sr. López compró este regalo para su esposa ayer.
Pedro	– Sr. López, ¿compró usted también discos en la tienda de Alberto?
Sr. López	– No, sólo la caja de música.
Sra. López	– Está muy bien, Carlos: en esta casa ya tenemos **demasiados** discos.

Juan Hoy, el Sr. López no compra discos.

Ayer, el Sr. López no compró discos.

Repita: hoy no compra – ayer no compró.

Ayer, el Sr. López no compró discos.

Conteste: ¿Qué compró?

Juanita – Compró una caja de música.

Juan ¿Compró la caja para su esposa o para su secretaria?

Juanita – Compró la caja para su esposa.

Juan ¿Cuándo compró este regalo, **la semana pasada** o ayer?

Juanita – Compró este regalo ayer.

Juan ¿Dónde compró el regalo?

Juanita – Compró el regalo en la tienda de Alberto.

demasiados discos – too many records. "Too many" is expressed by an adjective, which agrees in gender and number with the noun it modifies: **demasiado** (masculine) and **demasiada** (feminine) in the singular; **demasiados** and **demasiadas** in the plural.
When used with a verb, **demasiado** is an adverb meaning too (excessively) and has only one form. Ex.: **He comido demasiado.** – I've eaten too much.

¿Qué compró? – What did he buy? Notice that the 3rd-person preterite **compró** (bought) has a written accent on the last syllable to distinguish it from the 1st-person present **compro** (I buy).

la semana pasada – last week

Alberto la vendió. – Albert sold it.
la – it. Direct object pronoun, which in this case stands for **la caja** – the box.

Sra. López	– Alberto, esta caja de música (que usted **le vendió** a mi esposo) es muy bonita. Me gusta mucho.

Juan — *Conteste*: ¿Quién vendió la caja?

Juanita — – Alberto vendió la caja.

– Alberto la vendió.

– La vendió Alberto.

El Sr. López le da la caja. – Mr. López is giving her the box.
le – (to her). Indirect object pronoun, which in this case stands for **la esposa** – his wife.

dio – gave

Él no le dio ... – He didn't give her ...

Juan — Y hoy, el Sr. López da la caja **a su esposa:**

el Sr. López **le** da la caja.

Le da la caja para su aniversario.

Él no le **dio** la caja ayer: le da la caja hoy.

Escuche. No repita.

tomar un café, un chocolate – to drink (have) a cup of coffee, a cup of cocoa. As in English, **ch** is pronounced **tch;** the **e** is pronounced like the **e** in **bell.**

he comido y he bebido – I've eaten and I've drunk

Sr. López	– Yo tomo **un café** después de la cena.
Sra. López	– ¿Y usted, Sr. García? ¿Toma usted un café?
Sr. García	– Sí, con mucho gusto.
Sra. López	– ¿Y usted, Sra. García?
Sra. García	– No, gracias. Yo **he comido** y **he bebido** demasiado.

Pedro	– A mí **me gustaría tomar** un chocolate.
La madre de Pedro	– ¡Pedro!

me gustaría tomar – I would like to drink
We've already come across **me gusta** (I like) in the present tense. Here it's in the conditional, used the same as in English. It's a polite way to express a wish.

•••

FIN DE LA **ESCENA 21**

Exercise 21

1. Review of regular verbs in the imperative

		ESCUCH*AR*	APREND*ER*	ABR*IR*
¡Escuch*a*!	(tú)	¡Aprend*e*!	¡Abr*e*! (la puerta, etc.)
¡Escuch*e*!	(usted)	¡Aprend*a*!	¡Abr*a*!
¡Escuch*emos*!	(nosotros)	¡Aprend*amos*!	¡Abr*amos*!
¡Escuch*en*!	(ustedes)	¡Aprend*an*!	¡Abr*an*!

Ejemplo: ¡Ahora, muchachos y muchachas, *abran* sus libros, y *aprendan* los verbos! ¡*Estudien* el vocabulario y *hablen* claramente!

2. Reflexive verbs in the imperative

SENTARse (en una silla, etc.)

Ejemplos:

"Por favor, mamá, ¡*siéntate*!"
"Por favor, señor, ¡*siéntese*!"
"Ahora, todos nosotros, ¡*sentémonos*!"
"Por favor, señores, ¡*siéntense*!"

LEVANTARse (levantarse de la silla, levantarse de la mesa, ponerse de pie, etc.)

Ejemplos:

"Por favor, Pedrito, ¡*levántate*!"
"Por favor, señora, ¡*levántese*!"
"Ahora, todos nosotros, ¡*levantémonos*!"
"Por favor, señores, ¡*levántense*!"

Exercise 21

3. Placement of the objective personal pronoun used with the imperative

Usted toma *el libro*	= Usted *lo* toma	→ Por favor,	¡tóme*lo*!
Usted toma *la carta*	= Usted *la* toma.		¡tóme*la*!
Usted toma *los libros*	= Usted *los* toma.		¡tóme*los*!
Usted toma *las cartas*	= Usted *las* toma.		¡tóme*las*!

En el Imperativo afirmativo, los pronombres objetos se ponen después del verbo.

Usted abre *el libro*	= Usted *lo* abre.	→ Por favor,	¡ábra*lo*!
Ustedes hablan *este idioma*	= Ustedes *lo* habla.		¡háblen*lo*!
Usted aprende *la lección*	= Usted *la* aprende.		¡aprénda*la*!
Usted lee *los periódicos*	= Usted *los* lee.		¡léa*los*!
Ustedes venden *sus casas*	= Ustedes *las* venden.		¡véndan*las*!
Usted escribe a *su amigo*	= Usted *le* escribe.	→	¡Escríba*le*!

ESCENA 22

¿QUÉ TIEMPO HACE?

Sr. García	– ¡Oh, ya son las once!
Sra. García	– ¿Las once? ¿Ya?
El padre de Pedro	– Sí: ya es hora de **volver** a casa. Adiós, Sr. López. Adiós, Sra. López. Gracias por **todo.** ¡**Vámonos,** Pedro!
María	– Nosotros también **nos vamos.** Alberto, por favor, **mire por la ventana** para **ver** si llueve.
Alberto	– Ahora no llueve. **Hace buen tiempo.**

What's the Weather Like?

Ya son las once. – It's already eleven o'clock.
¿ya? – already?
Es hora de volver … – It's time to go back …
¡Vámonos! – Let's go! **Vamos,** the 1st-person plural imperative of **ir,** has lost its final consonant with the addition of the reflexive pronoun **nos.**
Nos vamos. – We're leaving (going away). Present indicative.
Mire por la ventana. – Look out the window. Imperative 3rd-person singular of **mirar** (polite **you**).
para ver si llueve – to see if it's raining
Hace buen tiempo. – The weather's fine.

buen – good. **Bueno** loses its final vowel when it's used before a singular masculine noun.

Juan	*Repita*: Alberto va a la ventana y **mira** por la ventana para ver si llueve.

Ya no llueve. – It isn't raining anymore. The root vowel of the verb **llover** changes from **o** to **ue** when it's stressed.
ya no – not anymore
Hace frío. – It's cold.
Here **hace** is the impersonal 3rd-person singular form of the verb **hacer** – do, make.
No hace calor. – It isn't hot. Literally: It doesn't make heat.

La madre de Pedro	– ¿Qué tiempo hace?
Alberto	– Hace buen tiempo. Ya no llueve.
La madre de Pedro	– Entonces, ¡vámonos!
Pedro	– Pero … ¡**hace frío**!¡Brrr!…
La madre de Pedro	– No, Pedro: no hace frío, **no hace calor,** no llueve. Hace un tiempo **espléndido …** Y ya es hora de volver a casa. ¡Vámonos!

Juan	*Repita la pregunta:* ¿Qué tiempo hace?
Juanita	*Repita la contestación*: – Hace buen tiempo.
Juan	*Conteste*: ¿Hace frío?
Juanita	– No, no hace frío.
Juan	¿Hace calor?
Juanita	– No, no hace calor.
Juan	¿Llueve?
Juanita	– No, no llueve.
Juan	*Repita la pregunta y la contestación:*

¿Llueve **todavía**? – No, **ya** no llueve.

todavía – still
¿Llueve todavía? – Is it still raining?

Alberto	– Vámonos.
María	– ¿En taxi?
Alberto	– No, **a pie**: ya no llueve. **El tiempo** está muy bueno: no hace frío y no hace calor.

Juan — *Repita*: **No** hace **ni** frío **ni** calor.

Ni frío ni calor.

Conteste: ¿Cómo **van** ellos, en taxi o a pie?

Juanita — – Van a pie.

Van a pie. – They're going on foot. They're walking. From the verb **ir.**

Alberto	– Buenas noches, Sr. López. Buenas noches, Sra. López. Gracias por la cena y por el concierto.
Sra. López	– Gracias a ustedes **por haber venido.**
Los padres de Pedro	– Gracias, y adiós.
Sr. López	– Adiós.
María	– Hasta mañana, Sr. López.
Sr. López	– Sí, **mañana es otro día ...** y tenemos **mucho que hacer** en la oficina. Hasta mañana, María.

por haber venido – for having come. Don't forget that the past participle never changes when used with **haber.**
Mañana es otro día. – Tomorrow is another day. **Otro** doesn't need the article **un** before it. This is also true of: **cierto** – certain; **medio** – half; **igual** – same; **tal** – such; and the adverb **tan** – so, as.
Tenemos mucho que hacer. – We have a lot to do.
Hasta mañana. – See you tomorrow. (Until tomorrow.)

Juan *Repita*: Mañana es sábado.

La oficina está **abierta** de nueve a doce.

desde ... hasta ... – from ... to ...
por la tarde – in the afternoon

Desde las nueve **hasta** las doce.

No está abierta **por la tarde.**

Sólo está abierta **por la mañana.**

Conteste: ¿A qué hora abre la oficina, a las siete **de la mañana** o a las nueve de la mañana?

abre – (it) opens

Juanita – La oficina abre a las nueve de la mañana.

cierra – (it) closes
a la seis de la tarde – at six o'clock in the evening

Juan ¿A qué hora cierra el sábado, a las doce o a las seis **de la tarde?**

Juanita – Cierra a las doce.

Juan ¿Y el domingo? ¿Está abierta la oficina el domingo?

Juanita – No, no está abierta el domingo.

¿cuántos días? – how many days?

Juan Recapitulación: ¿Cuántos días hay en una semana? – En una semana, hay ...

Juanita – En una semana, hay siete días.

Juan *Escuche. No repita.*

En una semana, hay siete días.

En **un año,** hay doce **meses.**

un año – one year
un mes, doce meses – one month, twelve months

Los meses del año son: **enero, febrero, marzo, abril, mayo, junio, julio, agosto, septiembre,**

octubre, noviembre, diciembre.

Ahora *conteste:* ¿Cuántos meses hay?

– Hay …

Juanita – Hay doce meses.

Juan *Repita los meses del año:*

Enero, febrero, marzo,

abril, mayo, junio,

julio, agosto, septiembre,

octubre, noviembre, diciembre.

hay – there is, there are. Impersonal 3rd-person singular of the verb **haber.** To express an amount of time that has passed, Spanish uses **hace.** Ex.: **hace cinco años** – five years ago.

•••

FIN DE LA **ESCENA 22**

Exercise 22

1. Negative forms in the present indicative and subjunctive

Usted no *nos* habla ⟶	Por favor, ¡no *nos* hable!
(Usted) no *me* escribe en inglés. ¡	¡No *me* escriba en inglés!
REFLEXIVOS: (Usted) no *se* sienta. ⟶	¡No *se* siente!
(Nosotros) no *nos* levantamos.	¡No *nos* levantemos!
(Ustedes) no *se* levantan.	¡No *se* levanten!

Regla: "Cuando el verbo está en el Imperativo NEGATIVO, la posición del pronombre objeto es la misma que en el PRESENTE negativo."

2. Vocabulary: the four seasons

¿Qué tiempo hace? ¿Cuál es la temperatura? ¿Cómo es el clima de su país?
En *primavera* y en *verano*, hace buen tiempo, hace sol, hace calor. En *otoño*, hace viento y llueve. En *invierno*, hace frío y nieva.

3. Simple past tense (preterite)

El "Pretérito perfecto" que estudiamos en el ejercicio 12 *no* es el único tiempo del pasado en español: para expresar el pasado, existe otro tiempo todavía *más* frecuente que el "Pretérito perfecto" del ejercicio 12: es el PRETÉRITO. El Pretérito es un tiempo que se usa muchísimo cuando queremos expresar las acciones del pasado. Estudie:

Hoy compro (*Presente* de "comprar") un disco. He comprado (*Pretérito perfecto*) muchos discos. Ayer, compré (*Pretérito*) un disco.

HABL*AR* **(Verbos regulares en el pretérito)**	BEB*ER*	ABR*IR*
(yo) habl*é*	beb*í*	abr*í*
(tú) habl*aste*	beb*iste*	abr*iste*
(él, ella, usted) habl*ó*	beb*ió*	abr*ió*
(nosotros, nosotras) habl*amos*	beb*imos*	abr*imos*
(vosotros, vosotras) habl*asteis*	beb*isteis*	abr*isteis*
(ellos, ellas, ustedes) habl*aron*	beb*ieron*	abr*ieron*

Exercise 22

4. Oral exercise

Conjugue oralmente en el Pretérito: LLAMAR (un taxi, por ejemplo), COMER (una fruta), RECIBIR (una carta).

CORRECCIÓN.

Yo llam*é*, tú llam*aste*, él llam*ó*, nosotros llam*amos*, etc. Yo com*í*, tú com*iste*, él com*ió*, etc. Recib*í*, recib*iste*, recib*ió*, etc.

ESCENA 23

ACTIVIDADES DIVERSAS **Various Activities**

Sr. López	– "A 30 de septiembre de 19 … Estimado señor, Esta carta es para **anunciar** a nuestros clientes, socios y empleados que el día martes, 4 de octubre, ……………………"	
Juan	*Conteste*: ¿Qué hace el director, lee la carta o	

To start a letter …
A 30 de septiembre de 19… – September 30, 19…
Estimado señor – Dear Sir
Esta carta es para … – This letter will … (The purpose of this letter is to …)
hace, lee, puede, tiene – 3rd-person singular of the verbs **hacer, leer, poder, tener** in the present tense

lee el periódico?

Juanita – Lee la carta.

podemos – we can. Verb **poder: puedo, puedes, puede, podemos, podéis, pueden.**

Juan *Repita*: **Él puede** leer la carta y nosotros podemos continuar: ¿Quién escribió **esa carta**, Pedro o María?

María la escribió. – María wrote it. **Escribió** is the simple past tense of the verb **escribir.** The simple past tense, or preterite, is used in Spanish very much as in English.

Juanita – María escribió esa carta.

Juan *Repita*: María **la** escribió.

¡Sí: la escribió María!

¿La escribió en inglés o en español?

Juanita – La escribió en español.

firmar – to sign

María	– Sr. López, usted tiene que **firmar** la carta.
Sr. López	– ¡Ah, sí! Tengo que firmar aquí …

Juan ¿Tiene María que firmar la carta?

Juanita – No, María no tiene que firmar la carta.

Juan ¿Quién tiene que firmar la carta, la secretaria o el director?

Juanita – El director tiene que firmar la carta.

Sr. López	– Firmo aquí.

firmo – I'm signing. **No firmo** – I'm not signing. Verb **firmar.**

Juan — *Conteste*: ¿Firma usted esa carta?

– No, yo no firmo ...

Juanita — – No, yo no firmo esa carta.

Juan — *Repita*: **Yo no he firmado** esa carta.

Conteste: ¿**Ha escrito usted** la carta?

– No, yo no he ...

Juanita — – No, yo no he escrito la carta.

Juan — ¿Quién ha escrito la carta?

Juanita — – María ha escrito la carta.

Juan — ¡Sí, María ha escrito o: María escribió la carta!

Escuche. Ahora María pone **las estampillas.**

Juan — *Escuche*. Ya son las cinco y cuarto.

María **ha llevado** todas las cartas al correo. Ahora **vuelve** a la oficina.

¿Firma usted? – Are you signing?

No he firmado. – I haven't signed.

Ha escrito. – She's written. Remember that the past participle never changes when used with the auxiliary **haber.** It must not be separated from its auxiliary. Ex.: **las cartas que hemos escrito** – the letters we've written.
He comido muy poco. – I've eaten very little.

escribió – she wrote. Simple past tense, or preterite.

ha llevado – she's taken. Verb **llevar.**
al correo – to the post office
las estampillas – stamps. In Spain, usually **los sellos.**
vuelve – she's coming back (to the office)

Sr. López	– ¿María?

Ya está. – That's it. All done.
ha llegado – has arrived. Verb **llegar.**

Hemos trabajado mucho. – We've done a lot of work. (We've worked a lot.) The Spanish adverb follows the past participle, which must never be separated from the auxiliary **haber.**
ya puede – now you can
irse – to leave (to go away). Verb **ir** (to go) + 3rd-person reflexive pronoun **se,** for polite **you.**
a su casa – home (to your house)
todavía no son ... – it isn't ... (time) yet
lo sé – I know
pero no importa – but it doesn't matter
Hemos trabajado bastante. – We've done enough work. Notice the adverb following the past participle.
sale de la oficina – she's leaving the office
salgo – I'm leaving (I'm going out); **sales** – you're leaving (singular familiar **you**); **sale** – he or she is leaving, you're leaving (**usted**)

María	– Ya está, Sr. López: he llevado todas las cartas al correo. ¡Ah! ... Y ha llegado este **telegrama**. Es para usted.
Sr. López	– Gracias. Hoy **hemos trabajado** mucho. Usted, María, ya puede **irse a su casa.**
María	– Pero ... todavía no son las seis; todavía no es hora de cerrar la oficina. Sólo son las cinco y cuarto ...
Sr. López	– Sí, lo sé. Pero **no importa**: Hemos trabajado **bastante** hoy. **Si** usted quiere, ya puede irse.
María	– Muchas gracias, Sr. López. Adiós.
Sr. López	– Hasta mañana.

Juan ¿Qué hace María, entra en la oficina o **sale** de la oficina?

Juanita – María sale de la oficina.

María	– Son las cinco y cuarto.

Juan *Repita*: Hoy María sale del trabajo a las cinco y cuarto.

Sale del trabajo y **se va** a su casa.

Pedro	– ¡María! ¿Se va usted?
María	– Sí, me voy.
Pedro	– Pero ... **no entiendo:** esta oficina cierra a las seis ... y ahora sólo son las cinco y cuarto.
María	– No importa. Me voy. Me voy a mi casa.
Pedro	– ¡María, **espere**! ¡Espere un momento! Yo también me voy. Me voy con usted.
María	– Bueno, **espero.** ¡Pero **venga pronto**!

No entiendo. – I don't understand.

¡Espere! – Wait!

¡Venga pronto! – Come on! Hurry up!

Juan — *Repita*: María **espera** a Pedro ...

Los minutos **pasan** ...

María espera, y espera, y espera ...

¡Y Pedro que no viene!

Espera a Pedro. – She's waiting for Pedro. Notice that the personal direct object is preceded by **a,** following the rule.
los minutos – the minutes. Note that **un segundo** means a second.
pasan – they're passing. **Pasar** is a regular verb, and so is **esperar.**

Pedro	– ¡Aquí estoy!
María	– ¡Por fin! ¡**Vámonos**!

Juan — Pedro y María **se van** juntos.

Juanita — ... Y nosotros también **nos vamos**. ¡Adiós!

¡Aquí estoy! – Here I am!
¡Por fin!– At last!
irse – to leave (to go away)

me voy	**nos vamos**
te vas	**os vais**
se va	**se van**

The pronoun **se** is added to the end of a verb in the imperative and in the infinitive:
¡Vámonos! – Let's go!
juntos – together
¡Adiós! Good-bye!

•••

FIN DE LA **ESCENA 23**

Exercise 23

1. Color nouns and adjectives

La leche es *blanca*. La nieve es blanca. El café solo es *negro*.
El blanco y el negro forman el *gris*. Cuando hace mal tiempo, el cielo está gris, y cuando hace buen tiempo, el cielo está *azul*.
El terreno de fútbol es *verde*. Las plantas del jardín son verdes.
El canario es *amarillo*. En Nueva York, los taxis son amarillos.
Los colores de la bandera española son: amarillo y rojo.

2. Opposites (antonyms)

El director *siempre* firma las cartas ... pero María no firma *nunca*.
La Sra. García quiere comer algo ... pero no quiere beber *nada*.
Ella come *mucho*, come *muchísimo* ... pero bebe poco, bebe *poquísimo*.
María va al cine con *alguien* ... pero el pobre Pedro no va con *nadie*.
(con Alberto) (Va solo)

3. Complete the sentences with a form of *tener*.

1. Es necesario telefonear: María ________________ que telefonear.
2. Es necesario repetir las frases: yo ________________ que repetir...
3. Es necesario saber los verbos: nosotros ________________ que saber...
4. Es importante estudiar: los estudiantes ________________ que estudiar.

4. Present and past tenses of the verbs *querer* (to love, to like), and *poder* (to be able)

Presente	*Pretérito perfecto*	*Pretérito*	*Presente*	*Pretérito perfecto*	*Pretérito*
quiero	he querido	quise	puedo	he podido	pude
quieres	has querido	quisiste	puedes	has podido	pudiste
quiere	ha querido	quiso	puede	ha podido	pudo
queremos	hemos querido	quisimos	podemos	hemos podido	pudimos
queréis	habéis querido	quisisteis	podéis	habéis podido	pudisteis
quieren	han querido	quisieron	pueden	han podido	pudieron

Exercise 23

CORRECCION.

1. Es necesario telefonear: *María tiene que telefonear.*
2. *yo tengo que repetir* 3. *tenemos que saber* 4. *tienen que estudiar.*

ESCENA 24

TRES AÑOS DESPUÉS, TRES AÑOS MÁS TARDE

Three Years Later

Juan — *Escuche. No repita.* El tiempo ha pasado … Ha pasado mucho tiempo … Tres años exactamente.
Han pasado tres años.
Pedro, María y el Sr. García ya no están en la oficina. Para saber dónde están nuestros amigos, vamos a escuchar una conversación

ya no están … – they're not … anymore

entre dos empleados de la oficina. Hablan de María.

casado, casada – married (masculine, feminine); **estar casado / a** – to be married (masculine, feminine)

un matrimonio muy feliz – a very happy couple (marriage). The form of **feliz** is the same for both masculine and feminine.
de vacaciones – on vacation

Un empleado	– Ahora, María está **casada.**
Otro empleado	– Sí! Ella y Alberto **forman** un matrimonio muy **feliz.** Ahora los dos están en Méjico. Están **de vacaciones** en Acapulco.

Juan — Ahora que María ya no está, el director no tiene secretaria.

no se quedaron – they didn't stay. Simple past tense of the verb **quedarse.**
se quedó – he stayed
nos quedamos – we stayed

Ha tenido dos o tres pero no se quedaron.

Y ahora no tiene ninguna secretaria.

Repita: No tiene ninguna.

buscar – to look for
alguien – someone
recomendar a alguien – to recommend someone. Note that the personal direct object is introduced by **a.**

Sr. López	– ¿Agencia Martín? Buenos días … **Buscamos** otra secretaria. **¿Puede usted recomendar a alguien**? ¿Hoy, no? ¿Pero mañana es **posible**? Bien, **llamaré** mañana. Adiós.

otra vez – one more time, again
Va a llamar otra vez. Llamará otra vez. – He's going to call again. He'll call again.

Juan — El Sr. López **va a llamar** otra vez.

Va a llamar otra vez mañana.

Repita: El Sr. López **llamará** otra vez mañana.

Un empleado – **Llamaremos** mañana, Sr. López.

Juan — *Repita* **el futuro** *del verbo "llamar":*

Yo llamar**é**, él llamar**á,**

nosotros llamar**emos,** ellos llamar**án.**

Un empleado	– ¡Sr. López! Es para usted.
Sr. López	– Gracias. ¿Sí? … ¿Quién habla?
María	– ¡Soy yo, Sr. López! ¿No me **reconoce**?
Sr. López	– ¡María! ¡Qué **sorpresa**! ¿Cómo está?
María	– Muy bien. ¿Ya tiene usted secretaria?
Sr. López	– No, todavía no: **no hemos encontrado** a nadie. No sé **lo que voy a hacer …**
María	– Yo tengo a una amiga que es secretaria. A ella le gustaría mucho trabajar para usted. **Si** usted me **permite**, yo quisiera recomendar**la.** ¿Puede ella **pasar** por su oficina para hablar con usted?
Sr. López	– ¡Cómo no, María! **Necesitamos** una buena secretaria. **Si** su amiga es **tan** buena secretaria **como** usted, yo la **contrataré** en seguida.
María	– ¡Estupendo! Ella **estará** muy **contenta.**
Sr. López	– Y nosotros aquí también **estaremos** muy **contentos.** ¿Cómo se llama su amiga?
María	– Se llama Carmen. Ella **pasará** por la oficina mañana por la tarde.
Sr. López	– ¡Perfecto! Yo la **esperaré** en mi oficina.
María	– Muy bien. Adiós, Sr. López.

The future of **llamar** – to call:

llamaré	**llamaremos**
llamarás	**llamaréis**
llamará	**llamarán**

No hemos encontrado a nadie. – We didn't find anyone (there).

Tengo a una amiga. – I have a friend (feminine).

Following the rule, the direct object is introduced by the personal **a,** which doesn't translate. We've already seen a number of examples.

si usted me permite – if you'll allow me. The construction is: **si** + present indicative of **permitir,** unlike the future in English.

recomendarla – to recommend her. **La** is the feminine direct object pronoun.

The conditional:

le gustaría – he or she would like

quisiera – I'd like. Verb **querer.**

Some verbs in the future indicative:

1st-person singular:

contrataré – I'll hire (under contract) (**contratar**)

esperaré – I'll wait (**esperar**)

tendré – I'll have (**tener**)

3rd-person singular:

tendrá – he'll have (**tener**)

estará – she'll be (**estar**)

pasará – she'll come by (**pasar**)

1st-person plural:

tendremos – we'll have

estaremos – we'll be

3rd-person plural:

tendrán – they'll have

tan … como – as … as

tan buena como usted – as kind (feminine) as you

un saludo a ... – say hello to ... (greetings for ...). This is an extremely useful expression for maintaining professional or friendly contacts.

Sr. López	– Adiós, María. Muchas gracias. ¡Y **un saludo** a Alberto!

Juan — *Repita*: Mañana, el director **tendrá** otra secretaria.

Repita el futuro del verbo "**tener**":

Yo **tendré**, él **tendrá**,

nosotros **tendremos,** ellos y ellas **tendrán.**

Sr. López	– ¡Mañana tendremos una **nueva** secretaria!

recomendó – she recommended. The personal **a** doesn't translate. Simple past tense.

la que viene – the one (feminine) who's coming
The terms **what** and **the one** (masculine or feminine), **who,** etc., are rendered in Spanish by the article, followed by **que.** Ex: **Haz lo que te digo** – Do what I say.
The one (masculine or feminine) **belonging to,** etc., is rendered in Spanish by the article followed by **de.** Ex: **No es tu oficina; es la del Sr. López.** – This isn't your office; it's Mr. López's (the one belonging to Mr. López).

Juan — ¿Quién **recomendó** a esa secretaria?

Juanita — – María recomendó a esa secretaria.

o: María la recomendó.

o: La recomendó María.

Un empleado	– ¿Cómo se llama la amiga de María?
Otro empleado	– ¿**La que viene** mañana?
El primero	– Sí, ¿Cómo se llama?

El segundo	– Carmen. **Dicen** que es muy bonita.
El primero	– ¿Qué edad tiene? ¿Es **joven**?
El segundo	– No sé, pero dicen que no está casada.
El primero	– ¡Ah! …

¿Cómo se llama? – What's her name?
Se llama Carmen. – Her name is Carmen.
dicen – they say, people say. Remember this impersonal "they."
Es bonita. – She's pretty.
joven – young (both masculine and feminine)
jóvenes – young people. The **v** is pronounced like a soft **b.**
ser and **estar:**
Es bonita. – She is pretty. A natural quality.
Está casada. – She is married. A permanent or temporary status.

Juan ¿Cómo se llama la **nueva** secretaria?

Juanita – Se llama Carmen.

Juan Así continua **la vida** en la oficina …

… ¡Y así termina nuestro programa!

Juanita **Estimados** señores, señoras, y señoritas, un millón de gracias por su atención!

estimados – dear (masculine plural). The adjective **querido / a** (dear, masculine and feminine) is used for relatives and close friends.

Juan ¡Y por su **buen** trabajo!

Juanita Adiós.

Juan Adiós … Y si va de vacaciones, **¡buen viaje!**

ir de vacaciones – to go on vacation
¡Buen viaje! – Have a good trip!

•••

FIN DE LA **ESCENA 24**

Exercise 24

1. Present progressive form (ESTAR + ...ando
ESTAR + ...iendo)

PRESENTE	FORMA PROGRESIVA DEL PRESENTE	
MIR**AR**	: Yo miro la televisión	= Yo estoy mir*ando* la televisión.
VEND**ER**	: Yo vendo mi casa	= Yo estoy vend*iendo* mi casa.
ESCRIB**IR**	: Yo escribo una carta	= Yo estoy escrib*iendo* una carta.

Otros ejemplos

Con el verbo TRABAJAR: Ahora Pedro *está trabajando* en una farmacia.
Con DAR: Ahora el profesor *está dando* clases en la universidad.
Con APRENDER: Los estudiantes *están aprendiendo* mucho.
Con HACER: Hoy *está haciendo* mucho calor.
Con LEER: Nosotros *estamos leyendo* esta página.
Etc...

2. Future indicative

	VIAJ**AR**	PERMIT**IR**	ENTEND**ER**
yo	viaj*aré*	permit*iré*	entend*eré*
tú	viaj*arás*	permit*irás*	entend*erás*
él (ella, usted)	viaj*ará*	permit*irá*	entend*erá*
nosotros (nosotras)	viaj*aremos*	permit*iremos*	entend*eremos*
vosotros (vosotras)	viaj*aréis*	permit*iréis*	entend*eréis*
ellos (ellas, ustedes)	viaj*arán*	permit*irán*	entend*erán*

Ejemplo: Hoy estoy en Chicago pero mañana *estaré* en Madrid.

Exercise 24

Some irregular verbs in the future indicative

TENER: ten*dré*, ten*drás*, ten*drá*, ten*dremos*, ten*dréis*, ten*drán*.
VENIR: ven*dré*, ven*drás*, ven*drá*, ven*dremos*, ven*dréis*, ven*drán*.

HACER: ha*ré*, ha*rás*, ha*rá*, ha*remos*, ha*réis*, ha*rán*.
DECIR: di*ré*, di*rás*, di*rá*, di*remos*, di*réis*, di*rán*.

Otros verbos irregulares en el futuro:

SABER (sa*bré*, sa*brás*, etc ...)
PONER (pon*dré*, etc ...); SALIR, contrario de "entrar" (sal*dré* ...);
PODER (po*dré*); QUERER (que*rré*), etc ...

3. Another past tense: the imperfect

Ejemplos: Cuando María trabaj*aba* de secretaria para el Sr. López, ella contest*aba* el teléfono y escribí*a* todas las cartas.
Cuando Pedro estudi*aba* español, él escuch*aba* las escenas, repetí*a* las frases, leí*a* el texto en el libro y hac*ía* todos los ..ejercicios.

	VISIT**AR**	COM**ER**	ABR**IR**
yo	visit*aba*	comí*a*	abrí*a*
tú	visit*abas*	comí*as*	abrí*as*
él (ella, usted)	visit*aba*	comí*a*	abrí*a*
nosotros (nosotras)	visitá*bamos*	comí*amos*	abrí*amos*
vosotros (vosotras)	visit*abais*	comí*ais*	abrí*ais*
ellos (ellas, ustedes)	visit*aban*	comí*an*	abrí*an*

Exercise 24

Some irregular verbs in the imperfect

IR: *iba, ibas, iba, íbamos, ibais, iban.*
SER: *era, eras, era, éramos, erais, eran.*
VER: *veía, veías, veía, veíamos, veíais, veían.*

Ejemplos: El año pasado, Pedro *iba* a la oficina todos los días.
María *era* la secretaria del Sr. López.
Alberto *veía* a María todos los sábados.

4. Dictation

To take dictation:
a) Listen to the beginning of scene 24 again.
b) Stop the cassette after the first sentence.
c) Write the sentence without looking at your book.
d) Listen to 2nd sentence, stop the cassette, write the sentence, and so on.

To correct the dictation: You can correct your dictation now by comparing it to the text in your book.

5. Complete each sentence with the verb shown, in the specified tense.

1. Ésta (SER, Presente) ________________ una recapitulación de los diversos tiempos que ustedes (ESTUDIAR, Pretérito) ________________.
2. Ayer, el Sr. López (HABLAR, Imperfecto) ________________ con sus empleados cuando María (TELEFONEAR, Pretérito) ________________.
3. La nueva secretaria (LLAMARSE, Presente) ________________ Carmen.
4. Carmen (LLEGAR, Futuro) ________________ mañana.
5. La Sra. López (TOCAR, Pretérito) ________________ la guitarra para sus invitados.
6. Todos los domingos, el Sr. y la Sra. López (JUGAR, Imperfecto) ________________ al tenis mientras el Sr. García (LEER, Imperfecto) ________________ el periódico en su casa.

Exercise 24

7. Por favor, señor, (ESCUCHAR, Imperativo)¡ ________________ las frases pero no las (REPETIR, Imperativo) —— en inglés!
8. Por favor, señoras y señores, (LEVANTARSE, Imperativo) ¡________________!
9. Ahora nosotros (CONTESTAR, Presente Progresivo, con "estar") ________________ las últimas preguntas del último ejercicio.
10. La semana que (VENIR, Presente) ________________, yo también (ESTAR, Futuro) ________________ de vacaciones en Acapulco. ¡Qué felicidad!

CORRECCIÓN en la página siguiente

6. Numbers

5: cinco
15: quince
50: cincuenta
51: cincuenta y uno
52: cincuenta y dos
53: cincuenta y tres

6: seis
16: dieciséis
60: sesenta
61: sesenta y uno
62: sesenta y dos
63: sesenta y tres

7: siete
17: diecisiete
70: setenta
71: setenta y uno
72: setenta y dos
73: setenta y tres

8: ocho
80: ochenta
81: ochenta y uno
82: ochenta y dos
83: ochenta y tres

9: nueve
90: noventa
91: noventa y uno
92: noventa y dos
93: noventa y tres

10: diez
100: cien
101: ciento uno
102: ciento dos
103: ciento tres

200: doscientos
201: doscientos uno
210: doscientos diez
215: doscientos quince
216: doscientos dieciséis
220: doscientos veinte

300: trescientos
400: cuatrocientos
500:quinientos
600: seiscientos
700: setecientos
900: novecientos

Exercise 24

1000: mil
1030: mil treinta
1900: mil novecientos
1989: mil novecientos ochenta y nueve

2000: dos mil
10 000: diez mil
70 000: setenta mil
100 000: cien mil
200 000: doscientos mil
1 000 000: un millón

CORRECCIÓN DEL EJERCICIO ANTERIOR.

1. Ésta es una recapitulación de los diversos tiempos que ustedes *estudiaron*.
2. Ayer, el Sr. López *hablaba* con sus empleados cuando María *telefoneó*.
3. La nueva secretaria *se llama* Carmen.
4. Carmen *llegará* mañana.
5. La Sra. López *tocó* la guitarra para sus invitados.
6. Todos los domingos, el Sr. y la Sra. López *jugaban* al tenis mientras el Sr. García *leía* el periódico en su casa.
7. Por favor, señor, ¡*escuche* las frases pero no las *repita* en inglés!
8. Por favor, señoras y señores, ¡*levántense*!
9. Ahora nosotros *estamos contestando* las últimas preguntas del último ejercicio.
10. La semana que *viene*, yo también *estaré* de vacaciones en Acapulco. ¡Qué felicidad!

GLOSSARY

A

a at, to 2
¿a qué hora? what time? 2
a las nueve at nine o'clock 2
vamos a ver we're going to see, we'll see 17
abierto open 17
abril april 20
abrir to open 10
absolutamente absolutely 19
absoluto absolute 19
en absoluto absolutely 19
nada en absoluto nothing at all 19
actividad activity 23
adiós good-bye 8
¿adónde? where to? where? 10
adulto adult, grownup 9
agosto August 22
ahora now 2
al - **a** + **el** 2
alemán German 14
alfabeto alphabet 15
algo something 19
alguien someone 9
almuerzo lunch 18
amable kind 15
amarillo yellow 23
América America 9
americano American 1
amiga friend (fem.) 17
amigo friend (masc.) 20
aniversario anniversary 20
antes de before 19
anunciar to announce 23
año year 22
¿cuántos años tiene? how old is he? 22
apellido last name, surname 10
aperitivo aperitif 19
aprender to learn 8
aprendido learned 12
aquello that 3
aquí here 5
por aquí through here 19
argentino / a Argentine 13
aritmética arithmetic 2
así like this 11
asistir to help 8
atención attention, kindness 20

por la atención for your kindness (in) 20
atentamente attentively 13
atento / a attentive 13
avenida avenue 8
aventura adventure 17
avión airplane 10
ayer yesterday 21
azul blue 23

B

bailado danced 20
bailar to dance 20
bandera flag 23
básico basic 3
basta that's enough! 3
bastante enough 23
beber to drink 20
bebido drunk 21
biblioteca library 17
bicicleta bicycle 1
bien well 2
bienvenido(s) welcome 19
bisté beefsteak 20
blanco white 23
bolígrafo (ballpoint) pen 11
bonito pretty 21
botella bottle 20
bravo bravo 5
buen good 22
buen viaje have a good trip 24
buenas noches good night 17
buenísimo very good, excellent 20
bueno (adj.) good 2
bueno (adv.) well 1
buenos días good morning 1
buscar to look for 12

C

café café, coffee 23
caja box 21
cajita little box 21
calor heat 22
hace calor it's hot 22
canario canary 23
canción song 5
cantar to sing 5
¡caramba! good grief! 10
carne meat 20
carta letter 9
casa house, home 7
casado / a married 24
cassette cassette 6
catedral cathedral 17
catorce fourteen 2
celebrar to celebrate 20
cena dinner, evening meal 18
cenar to eat dinner, dine 18
central central 8
cerca de near 12
cerrado closed 17
cerrar to close 2
cerveza beer 20
cielo sky 23
científicamente scientifically 13
científico / a scientific 13
cinco five 1
cincuenta fifty 5
cine movies 17
cita appointment, date 18
ciudad city 7
claramente clearly 7
claro of course 5
¡claro que sí! of course! 9
clase class 7
cliente client 23
clima climate 22
cocina kitchen 18
cóctel cocktail 19
coche automobile, car 1
Colombia Colombia 16
colombiano / a Colombian 18
color color 23
comenzar to begin 11
comer to eat 20
comida meal, food 18
comido eaten 21
comienza begins 16
como as, like 4
¿cómo? what did you say? 2
¿cómo está? how are you? 4
¡cómo no! of course! 6
tan ... como as ... as 24
cómodo comfortable 19
compañero companion 13
comprado bought 21
comprar to buy 17
comprender to understand 8
comprendido understood 12
computadora computer 10
con with 7
conducir to drive 15
conjugar conjugate 8
conocer to know, become acquainted with 18
contar to count 5
contento / a happy, pleased 24
contestación answer 13
contestar to answer 8
continuar to continue 11
contratar to hire (under contract) 24
conversación conversation 10
corrección correction 24
correctamente correctly 13
correcto correct 13
correo post office 23
correspondencia correspondence, mail 12

cortés courteous....13
cortesía courtesy....13
cortésmente courteously....13
cosa thing....15
costar to cost....11
cuál which, what....14
¿cuándo? when?....10
de cuando en cuando from time to time....18
¿cuánto dinero? how much money?....6
¿cuánto es? how much is it?....8
¿cuántos? how many?....22
cuarenta forty....5
cuarto quarter....23
y cuarto -fifteen....23
cuatro four....1
cuento I'm counting....5

CH

champán champagne....20
chocolate chocolate....21

D

dar to give....20
de from, of, belonging to....1
de ... a from ... to....5
¿de dónde? from where?....10
de nada you're welcome, it's nothing....5
de verdad really....14
decidido decided....12
decidir to decide....8
decir to say....2
defender to defend....11
del of the....3
delante in front (of)....12
delicado / a attentive, courteous....20
demasiado too (excessively)....13
demasiado/ a too many....21
demostrar demonstrate....11
derecha right....20
a la derecha on the right....20
desaparecer to disappear....15
desayuno breakfast....18
describir describe....8
desde from, since....22
desde ... hasta from ... to....22
después after....1
después de after....1
detrás de behind....12
día day....12
diccionario dictionary....11
dice says....17
diciembre December....22
dicho said (v. decir)....20
diecinueve nineteen....2
dieciocho eighteen....2
dieciséis sixteen....2
diecisiete seventeen....2
diez ten....2
difícil difficult....18
diga hello (say)....2
digo I say....24
dinero money....6
dio gave (v. dar)....21
dirección address....16
director manager, director....8
disco record....21
diverso / a various....23
divertido / a amusing....19
divertirse to have a good time....17
dividir to divide....8
diviértanse have a good time!....17
doble double....15
doce twelve....2
documento document....11
dólar dollar....3
domingo Sunday....16
don masculine title of respect....7
¿dónde? where?....8
dos two....1

E

edad age....24
ejemplo example....9
ejercicio exercise....13
el the....1
él he....4
ella she....4
ella (object) her....11
ellas they....10
ellos they....9
empezar to begin....11
empleado employee....18
en in, on....5
en el papel on the paper....12
¿en qué ...? in (on) what ... ?....7
en seguida right away....10
encantado / a pleased....19
encontrado found....12
encontrar to find....11
enero January....22
ensalada salad....20
entiendo I understand....19
entonces then....2
entrada entrance....19
entrar to come in, enter....1
es is....1
escena scene....1
escribir to write....9
escrito written....14
escuchado listened....19
escuchar to listen....7
escuela school....4
eso that....3
eso sí que no I should say not....16

esos those 5
ésos those (those ones)........................ 5
España Spain..................................12
español Spanish.................................4
esperar to wait, hope 20
espléndido splendid.........................22
esposa wife 18
esposo husband 21
está (he) is..4
  está bien that's all right 4
  ya está that's it, all done............19
ésta this (this one)..............................5
estamos we are 8
estampillas stamps (in Latin America)..................................23
  sellos stamps (in Spain) 23
estar to be 5
estará (he) will be............................24
éstas these (these ones)....................13
éste this (this one) 3
estimado dear 12
estimado señor dear sir 24
esto this 1
estos these 5
éstos these (these ones).......................5
estoy I am 10
estudiante student..............................4
estudiar to study 9
estupendo great 15
etc. etc. 12
exactamente exactly 5
exacto / a exact.................................13
excelente excellent..............................5
excepción exception..........................13
excepcionalmente exceptionally.....13
explicado explained..........................12
explicar explain 8

F

fácil 13
fácilmente easily 13
fantásticamente wonderfully...........13
fantástico fantastic, wonderful 13
farmacia pharmacy 24
favor favor...2
  por favor please 2
favorito / a favorite..........................20
febrero February 22
felicidad happiness 24
feliz happy 20
fiesta party...14
fin end 1
  por fin at last 10
firmado signed 23
firmar to sign 23
flor flower 20
forma form 10
formar to form 15
foto photograph 14
fotocopia photocopy 10
fotocopiar to photocopy 11
francés French 5
frase sentence 19
frecuente frequent 13
frecuentemente frequently 13
frío cold 22
  hace frío it's cold 22
fruta fruit..20
fútbol football, soccer.......................23

G

gato cat 3
general general 13
generalmente generally, usually 13
geografía geography 7
gobernar to govern 11
gracias thank you 1
gramática grammar 19
grande big 3
gris gray 23
guitarra guitar 24
gustar to please 20
  me gustan I like 20
gustaría would like............................21
  me gustaría I'd like.......................21
gusto pleasure 13
  con mucho gusto with great pleasure...20
  mucho gusto delighted, very pleased...13

H

ha (he) has (v. haber) 10
haber venido to have come 22
hablar to speak 9
  se habla is spoken 12
hacer to do, make 13
  hace buen tiempo the weather's fine 22
  hacer frío to be cold 22
hago I do, make 13
hasta until, up to 19
  hasta luego see you soon 16
  hasta mañana until tomorrow...22
hay there is, there are.......................16
hispano Hispanic 14
Hispanoamérica Latin America, Spanish America..........................14
hispanoamericano Latin American, Spanish American 14
hola hello, hi 4
hora time, hour 1
horrible horrible.................................13
horriblemente horribly 13
hoy today..16

I

identidad identity 14
idioma language 9
ido gone (v. ir) 17
importa it's important 23
  no importa it doesn't matter 23
importante important 19
independencia independence 16
infinitivo infinitive 8
inglés English 5
interesante interesting 19
invierno winter 22
invitación invitation 18
invitado invited 20
ir to go 10
irregular irregular 9
irse to leave, go away 23
Italia Italy 7
italiano Italian 5
-ito / a (diminutive suffix) 21
izquierda left 20
  a la izquierda on the left 20

J

japonés / japonesa Japanese 4
jardín garden 23
joven young 24
jueves Thursday 16
jugar to play 24
julio July 22
junio June 22
juntos together 10

L

la the 2
la (object) it 21
largo / a long 13
las the 1
lástima pity 6
  ¡qué lástima! what a pity! 6
le (presento) (let me introduce to) you (polite) 19
lección lesson 7
leche milk 20
leer to read 23
legumbres vegetables 20
leído read (v. leer) 20
lentamente slowly 13
libro book 13
lo it 4
  lo que what 13
  lo siento I'm sorry 4
los the 2
luego later 16
  hasta luego see you later 16
lunes Monday 16

LL

llamar to call 10
  ¿cómo se llama? what's her name? 13
  llaman a la puerta someone's knocking at the door 18
llamaré I'll call 24
llamarse to be named 14
llegado arrived 19
llegar to arrive 19
llevado brought, taken 23
llevar to bring, take 23
llueve it's raining 22

M

madre mother 18
¡madre mía! good grief! 16
magnífica magnificent 13
magníficamente magnificently 13
malamente badly 13
mantequilla butter 20
mañana tomorrow 22
  hasta mañana see you tomorrow 22
  por la mañana in the morning 16
máquina machine, typewriter 9
  escribir a máquina to type 9
maravillosamente marvelously 13
maravilloso / a marvelous 13
margarita daisy 20
martes Tuesday 16
marzo March 22
más more, plus 19
matrimonio marriage, couple 20
mayo May 22
me me, to me 13
medio half 22
  ocho y media eight-thirty 17
mediodía noon 18
mejicano Mexican 9
Méjico Mexico 14
menos less, minus 19
mes month 22
mesa table 12
metrónomo metronome 19
mi my 6
mí me 12
  delante de mí in front of me 12
miércoles Wednesday 16
mil thousand 11
millón million 24
minuto minute 2
mirar to look 17
mismo same 19
moderno modern 20
momento moment 18
motocicleta motorcycle 3
muchacha girl 18

muchacho boy 13
muchas gracias thanks a lot 2
muchísimo very, a great deal 17
  muchísimos coches a lot of cars 17
mucho / a a lot of 6
  mucho gusto very pleased, delighted 13
mujer wife, woman 18
mundo world 16
  todo el mundo everyone, the whole world 16
museo museum 12
música music 1
muy very 2

N

nada nothing 5
  de nada you're welcome, it's nothing 5
  no ... nada not ... anything 19
nadie no one 24
  no ... nadie not ... anyone 24
necesario necessary 23
necesitar to need 24
negativo negative 10
negro black 23
ni ... ni neither ... nor 16
  no ... ni ... ni ... not ... or ... or 16
nieva it's snowing 22
nieve snow 23
ninguno not one 24
niño child, little boy 9
no no, not 2
  no viene he's not coming 2
noche night 16
  buenas noches good night 17
nombre first name, given name 14
nosotras we (fem.) 8
nosotros we (masc.) 8
noviembre November 22
nuestro / a our 10
nueve nine 1
nuevo / a new 24
número number 2
nunca never 23
  no ... nunca not ever 23

O

o or 3
obedecer to obey 15
ocasión occasion 20
octubre October 22
ocupado busy 9
ocupar to occupy, keep busy 8
ocho eight 1
oficina office 10
oído heard (v. oír) 20
oigo I hear 19
oír to hear 20
omitir to omit 16
once eleven 2
otoño autumn 22
otro / a other, another 10
oye he hears 19

P

paciente patient 13
pacientemente patiently 13
padre father 18
padres parents 18
paella paella 20
página page 24
país country 7
pan bread 20
papel paper 12
para for 9
para (+ inf) to, in order to 11
parado stopped 10
  se ha parado it's stopped 10
parar to stop 13
particular particular 20
pasado past 21
  la semana pasada last week ... 21
pasaporte passport 14
pasar to pass 24
pausa pause 19
película film 17
pequeño / a small 3
perdón pardon, excuse me 1
perfectamente perfectly 13
perfecto / a perfect 4
periódico newspaper 21
permiso permission 19
  con permiso with (your) permission 19
permitir to allow 24
pero but 7
perro dog 3
persona person 9
pescado fish 20
peseta peseta 5
peso peso (Latin American monetary unit) 6
piano piano 3
pie foot 22
  de pie standing up 20
plantas plants 23
plato plate, dish 20
pobre poor 23
poco little 6
  poco a poco little by little 15
  un poco de a little 20
poder to be able 23
podido been able 23
policías police officers 17

poner to put 20
ponerse to become 14
poquísimo very little 23
por by, for 10
gracias por ... thank you for 10
por ahora for now 3
por aquí through here, this way 19
por favor please 2
por fin at last 10
por la mañana in the morning ..16
por la noche in the evening, at night 16
por la tarde in the afternoon, in the evening 16
por todas partes everywhere ...17
¿por qué? why? 13
porque because 13
posible possible 24
posición position 11
postre dessert 20
práctico / a pratical 13
preferir to prefer 11
pregunta question 13
preguntar to ask 14
preparado / a ready 11
preparar to prepare 18
presente present (now) 21
primavera spring 22
primero / a first 18
probable probable 13
probablemente probably 13
problema problem 19
producir to produce 15
profesor professor, teacher 1
programa program 24
progresos progress 15
prólogo prologue 1
prometer promise 8
pronto soon, quickly 19
hasta pronto see you soon 19
pude I could 23
puede he can 23
puerta door 3
pues well, then 5
pues sí well, yes 5
puesto put 20

Q

que who, which, that 2
lo que what 13
más ... que more ... than 19
menos ... que less ... than 19
qué which? what? 7
¡qué bonita! how pretty! 21
¿qué es esto? what's this? 3
¿qué hora es? what time is it? 1
¡qué lástima! what a pity! 6
¡que no! by no means! 7
quedar to stay 18
me quedo I'm staying 18
quedaron stayed 24
querer to like 17
queso cheese 20
¿quién? who? 4
quieto / a quiet 20
quince fifteen 2

R

radio radio 3
rápidamente rapidly, fast 13
rápido / a rapid 13
recapitulación recapitulation 10
recibir to receive 22
recomendar to recommend 24
reconocer to recognize 15
reflexivo / a reflexive 14
regalo gift 21
regular regular 14
reloj watch 1
repetir to repeat 2
resolver to resolve 11
restaurante restaurant 18
rojo / a red 23
rosa rose 20

S

sábado Saturday 16
saber to know 10
sacar to get, take out 17
sacar las entradas to get the tickets 17
salida exit 17
salir to leave, go out 18
salud health 20
¡salud! cheers! to your health! 20
saludo greeting 24
sangría sangria 19
se (reflexive or impersonal pronoun) 7
se habla español Spanish is spoken here 12
sé I know 3
secretaria secretary 4
seguida followed 10
en seguida right away 10
segundo second 23
seis six 1
semana week 16
la semana pasada last week ...21
sentado seated 20
sentarse to sit down 7
sentir to be sorry, regret 11
Señor / Sr. Mr. 4
el señor Nakamura Mr. Nakamura 4

Señor profesor Professor (respectful form of address) 2
los señores messieurs 10
señora Mrs. 4
las señoras mesdames.............10
señorita Miss 4
septiembre September 22
ser to be..4
si if 15
sí yes 1
eso sí que no by no means! 16
pero sí but I do (emphatic)..........16
siempre always...............................9
siéntese sit down 7
siento I'm sorry 4
siete seven 1
silencio silence 6
silla chair 19
sino but rather.................................20
situación situation 11
socio associate.................................23
sofá sofa 19
sol sun...22
hace sol it's sunny 22
solo / a alone 11
sólo only 6
somos we are 12
son they are.......................................1
sopa soup 20
sorpresa surprise 24
soy I am 4
su his, her; their; your **(de usted)** 6
sus their; your **(de ustedes)** 11

T

también also 4
tan so, as 13
tan ... como ... as ... as...........24
tan grande so big 18
tango tango 13
tarde afternoon, evening..................16
por la tarde in the afternoon, in the evening 16
taxi taxi 8
teatro theatre 15
telefoneado telephoned, called........19
telefonear to call on the telephone....17
teléfono telephone..........................12
telegrama telegram 23
televisión television 3
temperatura temperature 22
tendrá he'll have 24
tener to have.....................................6
tengo I have.......................................6
tengo que I have to, must 13
tenis tennis 24
terminado finished, over.................10
terminar to finish 16
terreno terrain..................................23
tiempo time 15
tiempo weather 22
¿qué tiempo hace? what's the weather like? 22
tiene he has, you (polite) have 6
tinto red (wine) 20
típicamente typically.......................13
típico / a typical 20
tocar to play (a musical instrument), touch 24
tocar la guitarra to play the guitar 24
todavía still, yet..............................15
todo all, everything 10
gracias por todo thank you for everything 22
todo el mundo everyone, the whole world..16
todos all, every (one).......................10
tomar to take, drink 19
trabajar to work.............................16
trabajo (n) work 16
traer bring 13
traído brought 20
trece thirteen...................................2
treinta thirty 5
treinta y uno thirty-one 5
tres three 1
tu, tus your 6
tú you...6

U

último,a last 24
un a, an (masc.) 1
una a, an (fem.) 1
universidad university 24
uno one 1
usted you (polite sing.) 4
ustedes you (polite plural)................11

V

va he's going 7
se va she's leaving 23
vacaciones vacation........................24
de vacaciones on vacation 24
vámonos let's go 22
veinte twenty....................................2
veintiuno twenty-one 5
vender to sell 21
vendió sold......................................21
Venezuela Venezuela.........................7
venga come 10
venir to come 10
ventana window 22
ver to see 17
verano summer 22
verbo verb 8
verdad truth 14

de verdad really 14
¿verdad? right?..........................7
verdaderamente really 13
verde green 23
vez time, occasion 24
viaje trip 24
buen viaje have a good trip 24
vida life 13
viene he's coming 2
viento wind......................................3
hace viento it's windy..............22
viernes Friday 16
vino wine 20
violín violin 3
visitado visited...............................12
visitar to visit....................................8
visto seen.......................................17
vocabulario vocabulary 3
volver to become, to return 22
voy I'm going 10
me voy I'm leaving 23

Y

y and 1
ya already 3
ya está that's it, all done.............6
yo I 4